BIRDS OF CONSERVATION CONCERN 2008

U.S. Fish and Wildlife Service
Division of Migratory Bird Management
Arlington, Virginia

December 2008

BIRDS OF CONSERVATION CONCERN 2008

Prepared by

U.S. Fish and Wildlife Service
Division of Migratory Bird Management
Arlington, Virginia

Suggested citation:
U.S. Fish and Wildlife Service. 2008. Birds of Conservation Concern 2008. United States Department of Interior, Fish and Wildlife Service, Division of Migratory Bird Management, Arlington, Virginia. 85 pp. [Online version available at <http://www.fws.gov/migratorybirds/>]

TABLE OF CONTENTS

LIST OF ACRONYMS

AI	Area Importance (an assessment factor)
ABC	American Bird Conservancy
BBS	Breeding Bird Survey
BCC	Birds of Conservation Concern
BCR	Bird Conservation Region
BD	Breeding Distribution
CCS	Continental Combined Score
DPS	Distinct Population Segment
ESA	Endangered Species Act
FWCA	Fish and Wildlife Conservation Act
MBTA	Migratory Bird Treaty Act
NABCI	North American Bird Conservation Initiative
NAWCP	North American Waterbird Conservation Plan
ND	Non-breeding Distribution
NWR	National Wildlife Refuge
PIF	Partners in Flight
PS	Population Size
PT	Population Trend
RD	Relative Density
TB	Threats in the Breeding Season
TN	Threats in the Non-breeding season
USFWS	U.S. Fish and Wildlife Service
USSCP	United States Shorebird Conservation Plan

EXECUTIVE SUMMARY

The 1988 amendment to the Fish and Wildlife Conservation Act mandates the U.S. Fish and Wildlife Service (USFWS) to "identify species, subspecies, and populations of all migratory nongame birds that, without additional conservation actions, are likely to become candidates for listing under the Endangered Species Act (ESA) of 1973." *Birds of Conservation Concern 2008* (*BCC 2008*) is the most recent effort to carry out this mandate. The overall goal of this report is to accurately identify the migratory and non-migratory bird species (beyond those already designated as federally threatened or endangered) that represent our highest conservation priorities. The geographic scope of this endeavor is the United States in its entirety, including island "territories" in the Pacific and Caribbean. *BCC 2008* encompasses three distinct geographic scales—North American Bird Conservation Initiative (NABCI) Bird Conservation Regions (BCRs), USFWS Regions, and National—and is primarily derived from assessment scores from three major bird conservation plans: the Partners in Flight North American Landbird Conservation Plan, the United States Shorebird Conservation Plan, and the North American Waterbird Conservation Plan.

Bird species considered for inclusion on lists in this report include nongame birds, gamebirds without hunting seasons, subsistence-hunted nongame birds in Alaska; and Endangered Species Act candidate, proposed endangered or threatened, and recently delisted species. Assessment scores from all three bird conservation plans are based on several factors, including population trends, threats, distribution, abundance, and relative density. These assessment scores serve as the foundation on which we built the *BCC 2008* lists. Although the different bird conservation plans use somewhat different methods for determining the highest priority species, the scores from each represent true conservation priorities for each of the three species groups (landbirds, shorebirds, and waterbirds). We therefore view the conservation priorities within each plan as approximately equivalent. After creating BCR lists, we developed specific criteria for including species on USFWS Region and National lists. The various BCR lists contain 10 to 53 species, USFWS Region lists contain 27 to 78 species, and the National list contains 147 species. On average, priority species make up about 10 to 15 percent of the native bird species in any given geographic unit.

While all of the bird species included in *BCC 2008* are priorities for conservation action, this list makes no finding with regard to whether they warrant consideration for ESA listing. Our goal is to prevent or remove the need for additional ESA bird listings by implementing proactive management and conservation actions. We recommend that these lists be consulted in accordance with Executive Order 13186, "Responsibilities of Federal Agencies to Protect Migratory Birds." This report should also be used to develop research, monitoring, and management initiatives. *BCC 2008* is intended to stimulate coordinated and collaborative proactive conservation actions among Federal, State, Tribal, and private partners. We hope that, by focusing attention on these highest-priority species, this report will promote greater study and protection of the habitats and ecological communities upon which these species depend, thereby contributing to healthy avian populations and communities.

ACKNOWLEDGMENTS

This document was the result of close collaboration between staff in all regions of the U.S. Fish and Wildlife Service's Migratory Bird Program. The primary collaborators were Mila Plavsic, Jeff Shenot, and Marie Strassburger (Region 9); the initiative coordinators, Brad Andres (U.S. Shorebird Conservation Plan; USSCP), Jennifer Wheeler (North American Waterbird Conservation Plan; NAWCP) and Terry Rich (Partners in Flight; PIF); and the Regional Coordinators: Tara Zimmerman, Mike Green, Nanette Seto, Sue Thomas, and Maura Naughton (Region 1), Bill Howe and Dave Krueper (Region 2), Steve Lewis, Tom Will, and Bob Russell (Region 3), Dean Demarest, Chuck Hunter, Jaime Collazo, and Stefani Melvin (Region 4), Randy Dettmers (Region 5), Stephanie Jones, Suzanne Fellows, and Kevin Kritz (Region 6), Kent Wohl, Steve Matsuoka, and Richard Lanctot (Region 7). All were involved in developing selection criteria, compiling and finalizing BCR and USFWS Region lists, and reviewing and commenting on several drafts of this report.

The basis of this list is the work that many people have done to reach true avian priorities, and we have based this document on their work. We are particularly grateful for all of the work the initiatives (USSCP, NAWCP, and PIF) have done completing prioritization scores and methods. We thank Arvind Panjabi (Rocky Mountain Bird Observatory) for making available the PIF database and for responding to our many questions.

This edition of the *BCC 2008* is dedicated to John L. Trapp, who retired from USFWS in 2007 after 33 years of outstanding contributions to bird conservation. John had an extensive ornithological knowledge and passion for birds, and he oversaw almost all of the previous editions of the Birds of Conservation Concern.

INTRODUCTION

The purpose of this document is to identify migratory and non-migratory birds of the United States and its territories that are of conservation concern so as to stimulate coordinated and proactive conservation actions among Federal, State, Tribal, and private partners. The conservation concerns may be the result of population declines, naturally or human-caused small ranges or population sizes, threats to habitat, or other factors. The primary statutory authority for *Birds of Conservation Concern 2008 (BCC 2008)* is the Fish and Wildlife Conservation Act of 1980 (FWCA), as amended; other authorities include the Endangered Species Act (ESA) of 1973, the Fish and Wildlife Act of 1956, and 16 U.S.C. § 701. The 1988 amendment (Public Law 100-653, Title VIII) to the FWCA requires the Secretary of the Interior, through the United States Fish and Wildlife Service (USFWS), to "identify species, subspecies, and populations of all migratory nongame birds that, without additional conservation actions, are likely to become candidates for listing under the Endangered Species Act of 1973." *BCC 2008* is the most recent effort by the USFWS to carry out this proactive conservation mandate and update *Birds of Conservation Concern 2002* (USFWS 2002). The overall goal of this report is to accurately identify those species (beyond those already federally listed as threatened or endangered) in greatest need of conservation action at three different geographic scales.

A primary goal of the USFWS is to conserve avian diversity in North America (USFWS 1990, 2004). This goal includes reducing or removing threats that may necessitate that a species be considered for listing under the ESA. The Birds of Conservation Concern are largely a subset of a larger list known as the Birds of Management Concern (BMC). The BMC is a subset of all species protected by the Migratory Bird Treaty Act (MBTA, see 50 CFR 10.13), and includes those which pose special management challenges due to a variety of factors (e.g., too few, too many, conflicts with human interests, or societal demands) (USFWS 2004). The BMC includes both game birds below their desired condition and nongame birds. As indicated in its strategic plan (USFWS 2004), the Migratory Bird Program places priority emphasis on these birds in its activities.

The philosophy underlying this report is that proactive bird conservation is necessary at a time when human impacts are at an all-time high. We strongly believe that a well-designed program that addresses resource-management issues up front will prevent or remove the need to consider listing species as threatened or endangered, and will promote and conserve long-term avian diversity in the United States. In addition, proactive conservation clearly is more cost-effective than the extensive recovery efforts required once a species is federally listed under the ESA. Our intent is for *BCC 2008* to stimulate coordinated efforts to develop and implement comprehensive and integrated approaches for the study, management, and protection of "non-ESA listed" bird species deemed to be in the most need of additional conservation actions. It should also be noted that, while the inclusion of native species not listed under the MBTA is beyond the scope of the FWCA, the USFWS has an incentive to encourage proactive management of these species by State agencies and other partners to prevent the need for listing them as endangered or threatened.

Bird species assemblages, guilds, or communities have recently been promoted as indicators of ecological integrity in a variety of habitats (Bradford et al. 1998, O'Connell et al. 2000, Canterbury et al. 2000, Venier and Pearce 2007), and at-risk bird species are good measures of ecosystem threats (Beissinger et al. 1996). Setting priorities in conservation is crucial because resources are limited. Many systems for setting wildlife-conservation priorities have been proposed. Some have focused heavily on identifying and quantifying threats to endangered or rare species (Master 1991, Wilcove et al. 1998). Others have focused on highlighting species that deserve attention due to threats to their populations, widespread or long-term declines, or low potential for population recovery (Millsap et al. 1990). The Canadian Wildlife Service developed a priority ranking system that focuses on conservation concerns and agency responsibilities to assist in setting conservation priorities for landbird species (Dunn 1997, Dunn et al. 1999). The mandate of the 1988 FWCA amendment requires a more proactive approach.

BCC 2008 uses current conservation assessment scores from three bird conservation plans: Partners in Flight North American Landbird Conservation Plan (PIF; Rich et al. 2004), the United States Shorebird Conservation Plan (USSCP; Brown et al. 2001, USSCP 2004), and the North American Waterbird Conservation Plan (NAWCP, Kushlan et al. 2002). Waterfowl game species covered by the North American Waterfowl Management Plan (Canadian Wildlife Service, U.S. Fish and Wildlife Service, Secretario de Medio Ambiente y Recursos Naturales, 2004) are specifically excluded from the BCC list in accordance with the FWCA of 1980. Species in need of additional conservation attention are identified at three distinct geographic scales: North American Bird Conservation Initiative (NABCI) Bird Conservation Regions (BCRs; U.S. NABCI Committee 2000a, 2000b, 2000c), USFWS Regions, and National.

Assessment scores are based on several parameters including population trend, threats, distribution, abundance, and the importance of an area to a species. Partners in Flight, a coalition of Federal and State government agencies, non-governmental organizations, and private interests, developed species assessment scores out of concern for the sharp declines in many North American landbirds (Rich et al. 2004). The PIF approach (Carter et al. 2000, Rich et al. 2004) has been peer-reviewed by an independent body of avian biologists (Beissinger et al. 2000). Similar coalitions have prepared and reviewed conservation assessment scores for shorebirds at the National scale (Brown et al. 2000, USSCP 2004), and in step-down regional shorebird conservation plans (see http://www.fws.gov/shorebirdplan) and for waterbirds at the continental scale (Kushlan et al. 2002) and in step-down regional waterbird conservation plans (see http://www.waterbirdconservation.org). Additionally, we found it necessary to develop conservation assessment scores for species not yet evaluated by any of the bird conservation plans, such as Pacific Island birds. Taken together, these assessment scores can be used to develop a comprehensive set of integrated bird conservation priorities; this represents a unique conservation effort unmatched in any other major group of organisms in North America.

BACKGROUND

Why Did We Create Lists at Different Geographic Scales?

Listing birds of conservation concern at three geographic scales maximizes the utility of the lists for a variety of partner agencies and organizations. The different geographic scales, from smallest to largest, are as follows:

Bird Conservation Regions (BCRs). We have adopted BCRs as the smallest of our geographic scales. BCRs have been endorsed by the North American Bird Conservation Initiative (NABCI, U.S. NABCI Committee 2000a, 2000b, 2000c) as the basic units within which all-bird conservation efforts will be planned and evaluated (Fig. 1). The NABCI is an endeavor to increase the effectiveness of bird conservation at the continental level and currently includes the United States, Canada, and Mexico. Its goal is to deliver "the full spectrum of bird conservation through regionally based, biologically driven, landscape-oriented partnerships" (U.S. NABCI Committee 2000a). A published map of BCRs and accompanying written descriptions of each are available (U.S. NABCI Committee 2000b, 2000c). The BCR lists will be most useful to Federal land-managing agencies and their partners in their efforts to abide by the bird conservation principles embodied in the MBTA and Executive Order 13186, "Responsibilities of Federal agencies to protect migratory birds" (Clinton 2001). The NABCI has recognized 35 BCRs that cover the contiguous 48 States, Alaska, and Hawaii, numbered 1 to 5, 9 to 37, and 67 (Hawaii) (U.S. NABCI Committee 2000a, 2000b, 2000c, http://www.nabci-us.org/bcrs.html). For purposes of this report, we created two additional BCRs to encompass island "territories" of the United States,[1] "Other U.S. Pacific Islands" (i.e., excluding Hawaii) and "U.S. Caribbean Islands." In the *BCC 2002* report, these two BCRs were referred to as BCR 68 for the Pacific Ocean and BCR 69 for the Caribbean, but those designations were changed for *BCC 2008* because NAWCP uses those numbers to refer to marine areas ("pelagic" BCRs). Although *BCC*

---

[1] Island "territories" and other affiliations of the United States considered in this document include (a) *American Samoa*—an unincorporated and unorganized territory; (b) *Baker Island*—an unincorporated territory administered by the USFWS as a National Wildlife Refuge (NWR); (c) *Commonwealth of the Northern Marianas Islands*—aligned through a covenant of "political union"; (d) *Guam*—an unincorporated organized territory; (e) *Howland Island*—an unincorporated territory administered by the USFWS as a NWR; (f) *Jarvis Island*—an unincorporated territory administered by the USFWS as a NWR; (g) *Johnston Atoll*—an unincorporated and unorganized territory under joint operational control of the Department of Defense and USFWS (and administered as a NWR); (h) *Kingman Reef*—an unincorporated territory administered by the USFWS as a NWR; (i) *Midway Atoll*—an unincorporated territory administered by the USFWS as a NWR; (j) *Navassa Island*—administered by the USFWS as a NWR; *(k) Palmyra Atoll*—an incorporated territory that is partially privately owned and partially administered by USFWS as an NWR; (l) *Commonwealth of Puerto Rico*—a commonwealth; (m) *U.S. Virgin Islands*—an unincorporated organized territory; and (n) *Wake Island*—an unincorporated territory administered by the Department of the Interior (Central Intelligence Agency 2001).

2008 does not adopt the pelagic BCR system, it recognizes that some BCC species occur in the U.S. primarily or only at sea. These species are listed under the adjacent terrestrial BCR. Thus, there are 37 BCR lists of priority species.

USFWS Regions. BCC lists are presented in this document for 8 USFWS Regions.[2] The USFWS Region lists will be useful to USFWS administrators and biologists, other Federal and State agencies within a Region, and their partners and cooperators.

National. The National list encompasses the United States in its entirety, including island "territories" in the Caribbean and the Pacific. The National list should be viewed as a barometer of the status of U.S. bird populations, providing an "early warning" of birds that may decline to levels requiring ESA protection unless additional conservation measures are taken. The National list will be most useful as an outreach tool for educating the public about the precarious status of bird species in the U.S. It will also be useful for National bird conservation planning. The National list should not be used to foster bird conservation at smaller geographic scales; that is the purpose of the BCR and USFWS Region lists.

Although there are other lists of this nature, such as the National Audubon Society/American Bird Conservancy 2007 WatchList (Butcher et al. 2007), *BCC 2008* is the only list that meets USFWS mandates for the conservation of migratory nongame birds. Conservation organizations create lists of concern that reflect their unique missions, and it is important to keep this in mind when comparing lists. With regard to birds, the USFWS focuses on its trust responsibilities as defined by the Code of Federal Regulations, which excludes, for example, gallinaceous birds (resident game birds) unless they are listed as threatened or endangered under the Endangered Species Act (ESA). Similarly, the *Birds of Conservation Concern*, as mandated by Congressional legislation, excludes birds regulated as hunted species and birds listed under the ESA. Nongovernmental organizations like American Bird Conservancy (ABC) or National Audubon are not limited by these legal distinctions, and as a result they can provide lists that are more inclusive. The USFWS *Birds of Conservation Concern*, the ABC/Audubon Watch List, and a number of other lists share a common base: they are all reliant on the conservation assessments of the major bird partner initiatives and the surveys upon which those initiative assessments are grounded. National Audubon, American Bird Conservancy, and the USFWS are all partners, among others, in participating in the assessments of those initiatives.

---

[2] The Pacific Region (Region 1) includes Idaho, Oregon, Washington, Hawaii, and the Pacific Islands. The Southwest Region (Region 2) includes Arizona, New Mexico, Oklahoma, and Texas. The Great Lakes-Big Rivers Region (Region 3) includes Illinois, Indiana, Iowa, Michigan, Missouri, Minnesota, Ohio, and Wisconsin. The Southeast Region (Region 4) includes Alabama, Arkansas, Florida, Georgia, Kentucky, Louisiana, Mississippi, North Carolina, Puerto Rico/Virgin Islands, South Carolina, and Tennessee. The Northeast Region (Region 5) includes Connecticut, Delaware, Maine, Maryland, Massachusetts, New Hampshire, New Jersey, New York, Pennsylvania, Rhode Island, Vermont, Virginia, and West Virginia. The Mountain-Prairie Region (Region 6) includes Colorado, Kansas, Montana, North Dakota, Nebraska, South Dakota, Utah, and Wyoming. The Alaska Region (Region 7) consists of the state of Alaska. The California and Nevada Region (Region 8) consists of the states of California and Nevada.

What Bird Species Did We Consider?

The various species groups considered for inclusion in *BCC 2008* are described in Table 1 and include nongame birds; gamebirds without hunting seasons; subsistence-hunted nongame birds in Alaska; and Endangered Species Act candidate, proposed endangered or threatened, and recently delisted species. The major groups of species not considered in this assessment are (1) migratory gamebirds for which hunting regulations are established (i.e., cooperatively managed by Federal-State flyway councils); (2) species that are peripheral to the U.S. (i.e., population fragments within U.S. jurisdiction are too small to be managed capably); (3) species, subspecies, and populations of federally-endangered or -threatened birds (i.e., those subject to the provisions of the ESA); (4) resident gamebirds (i.e., managed by State wildlife agencies), unless listed as a federal ESA candidate; and (5) non-native species.

Because the assessments of the three bird conservation initiatives that we use here are all species-based, assessment scores were available only for full species. However, where appropriate, subspecies and populations are included in this assessment based on geographic range, federal candidate status, or available local data. Such subspecies and populations are noted on lists at all three geographic scales.

In the spirit of all-bird conservation, we include native species not specifically covered by the MBTA when they are deemed to be conservation priorities, as long as they are not part of one the groups excluded from consideration (see above). To avoid confusion, we clearly differentiate between those species that are and are not protected by the MBTA. A list of species protected by the MBTA is found in Title 50, Part 10, of the *Code of Federal Regulations*.

What Sources of Information Did We Use?

The methods used to assess and prioritize species differ between PIF, the USSCP, and the NAWCP. These differences relate to geographic scope, factor thresholds, and treatment of uncertainty. Although the methods for determining the highest-priority species are somewhat different among the different initiatives, scoring reflects state-of-the-art conservation assessments for each of the three species groups (landbirds, shorebirds, and waterbirds); we therefore view the conservation priorities within the three conservation plans as approximately equivalent.

PIF Assessment Scores. We used assessment scores from the PIF Species Assessment Database (version 2005, with unpublished 2007 updates) housed at the Rocky Mountain Bird Observatory, which we believe were the best available data at the time this report was prepared. In this database a panel of bird species experts has assigned each landbird species in North America scores ranging from 1 (lowest priority or degree of concern) to 5 (highest priority or degree of concern) for each of six factors, assessing aspects of future vulnerability at the range-wide scale: Population Size (PS), Breeding Distribution (BD), Non-breeding Distribution (ND), Threats in the Breeding Season (TB), Threats in the Non-breeding season (TN), and Population Trend (PT) (Panjabi et al. 2005). These factors are then used to calculate a Continental Combined Score

(CCS): PS + max(BD, ND) + max(TB, TN) + PT. The threats scores and the distribution scores are highly correlated so PIF used this score rather than a simple total. Thus, CCS ranges from 4 for a widespread and increasing species which is expected to face even more favorable conditions in the future, to 20 for a species of the very highest future conservation concern. The CCS was used to develop the landbird portion of the National BCC list.

Partners in Flight also assesses species at the BCR level. That assessment includes two additional criteria, Relative Density (RD) and Percent of Population, which reflect the importance of a particular BCR to each species. The global scores for TB, TN, and PT are also adjusted using BCR-specific data. These BCR scores informed the selection of landbirds for the *BCC 2008* BCR lists.

All of these factors are defined and discussed in detail in Panjabi et al. (2005). Both PIF breeding and wintering (non-breeding) scores, where available, were used in assessing species for inclusion in the *BCC 2008* report. In consultation with experts, the USFWS prepared scores for landbirds of Hawaii and Pacific island "territories" using the PIF process.

USSCP Assessment Scores. For shorebird species, we started with the updated assessment scores from the USSCP (USSCP 2004), which were built on original plan assessments (Brown et al. 2000, Brown et al. 2001). We incorporated new information on shorebird population trends and sizes published by Morrison et al. (2006) and Bart et al. (2007). Information on population sizes were ranked according to the PIF criteria. We also included updates in breeding and nonbreeding threats provided by regional shorebird working groups. The USSCP assessment process uses most of the same factor scores (with slightly different criteria) as PIF, but priorities were derived using a categorical (rather than a summation) approach (Brown et al. 2001). A prioritization protocol for shorebirds (in Brown et al. 2001) describes prioritization categories and their relationship to factor scores.

NAWCP Assessment Scores. Like USSCP, the NAWCP assessment process also uses most of the same factor scores (with slightly different criteria) as PIF and derives priorities using a categorical approach (Kushlan et al. 2002). For all three scales used in the BCC, we referred to the continental-scale assessment results documented in the NAWCP plan (Kushlan et al. 2002) and subsequent analyses (i.e., for non-colonial waterbirds, documented at http://www.waterbirdconservation.org), which we considered to be the best available data for waterbirds and seabirds. For *BCC 2008* BCR lists, we also referred to assessments in regional waterbird conservation plans or documents that most closely resemble regional waterbird conservation plans, where available (see www.waterbirdconservation.org.) These regional-scale status assessments are, in general, based on the continental-scale assessment, though regional planning groups made adjustments based on BCR-scale needs and values.

What Selection Criteria Did We Use For *Birds of Conservation Concern 2008* Lists?

The following are the criteria used to select species for consideration and inclusion on BCR, USFWS Region, and National lists. At each scale, USFWS expertise and discretion refined the pool of species under consideration from the three bird conservation initiatives—as well as those selected for priority lists—to comply with the FWCA amendment of 1988. The same criteria were used for all subspecies and populations considered separately for inclusion.

There may be additions to the lists over the next several years. Newly designated Federal candidate species, species proposed for listing, and species removed from the list of endangered and threatened species will automatically be considered to be on the appropriate BCC list(s), effective the day of their designation or delisting as published in the *Federal Register*.

General criteria (rule-sets) for placing species on any BCC list

1. Begin with list from appropriate bird conservation initiative.

2. Follow criteria below for appropriate bird groups (see Panjabi et al. 2005 for explanation of terms).

3. Add non-breeding species if the species occurs at significant Relative Density scores and/or has moderate or high threat levels (based on expert opinion or data) in non-breeding season, if not already included due to breeding population (indicate with "nb").

4. Consider subspecies and populations where appropriate and where information on their status is available (e.g., Dickinson 2003).

5. Remove sport-hunted species (including their non-hunted populations) and federally-listed threatened or endangered populations (retaining non-listed populations with notation).

6. Add any recently ESA de-listed, candidate, or proposed species not already included.

7. In very limited circumstances, add or remove species (and document rationale) when Service expertise, supplemental information, or local data indicates a much greater or lesser degree of concern than that reflected by bird conservation initiative scoring.

Criteria for placing species on BCR lists

LANDBIRD criteria for *BCR* lists (see Panjabi 2005 for explanation of terms):

1. Include species meeting the PIF criteria for Species of Regional Importance – Continental Concern (U.S. and Canada), EXCEPT

   a) if Regional Combined Score <15 and Action Code = "Planning and Responsibility"

   b) in BCRs shared with Canada and Mexico, those with Relative Density ≥1 in the *U.S.* portion of the BCR (consult state population data).

c) for species shared with Latin America and the Caribbean (LAC), remove species with core ranges outside the U.S. and its territories if <1% of population or range-wide distribution is in the U.S. and threats in LAC are low. However, if conservation action for a species is warranted in the U.S. due to high threats in LAC, then it could be included in the appropriate U.S. BCR lists.

2. Include species meeting the PIF criteria for Species of Regional Importance – Regional Concern IF:

   a) Regional Combined Score $\geq$15 and Action Code = "Critical Recovery" or "Immediate Management"

   b) Regional Combined Score $\geq$ 17 and Action Code = "Management Attention"

3. Rank species in Hawaii and Pacific island territories using latest PIF criteria and above criteria as appropriate.

SHOREBIRD criteria for *BCR* lists:

1. Include all species, subspecies, and populations meeting criteria for National BCC List if >1% of taxon occurs anytime during annual cycle in the BCR (i.e., Relative Density $\geq$1 in the BCR). The criteria for National BCC List are:

   a) population is undergoing a strong decline (Population Trend = 5), regardless of population size; OR
   b) population is declining or stable (Population Trend = 4 or 3) and populations are small, distributions are limited and threats are high (Population Size + Breeding Distribution + Non-breeding Distribution + Threats to Breeding + Threats to Non-breeding $\geq$ 18).

WATERBIRD criteria for *BCR* lists:

1. Initially identify species of greatest concern from each BCR using the regional waterbird conservation plans or similar documentation (e.g., Joint Venture implementation plans). Depending on BCR-scale approaches, include species regionally assessed as High or Highest/Highly Imperiled, as Tier I (if the PIF approach was used), or priority species for BCR-scale partnership.

2. Remove species from BCR lists if U.S. populations are considered unmanageable (e.g., Relative Density <1).

3. Identify and retain only those species of greatest conservation concern, as some regional-plan species lists were designed to maximize support for a wide range of conservation activities by partners or identify species around which partnerships could operate.

Criteria for placing species on USFWS Regional lists

1. Include species from the BCC BCR lists if the species has the equivalent of a RD >1 or a manageable population in 50% or more of the BCRs in which it occurs within a USFWS region.

Criteria for placing species on BCC National list

LANDBIRD criteria for *National* list:

1. Include all PIF "Continental Watchlist" (which includes the U.S. and Canada) species and U.S. island territories' species that meet PIF Continental Watchlist criteria EXCEPT,

   a) species without manageable populations in the U.S. or its territories; however, if conservation action is warranted in the U.S. due to high threats elsewhere, then such species could be included;

   b) species that are not listed on any BCC BCR list.

SHOREBIRD criteria for *National* list:

1. Include species (or subspecies/population designations where supported by USSCP Conservation Assessment [2000] or more recent work) that meet any ONE of the following criteria:

   a) population is undergoing a strong decline (Population Trend = 5), regardless of population size; OR
   b) population is declining or unknown (Population Trend = 4 or 3) and populations are small, distributions are limited and threats are high (Population Size + Breeding Distribution + Non-breeding Distribution + Threats to Breeding + Threats to Non-breeding $\geq$ 18).

Scores have been revised and reflect the best science to date and are under review (Andres unpubl.).

WATERBIRD criteria for *National* list:

1. Include species ranked "Highly Imperiled" in the NAWCP continental-scale assessment unless not occurring on any BCR list.

2. Consider all species ranked "High" in the NAWCP continental-scale assessment (unless not

---

occurring on any BCR list) and include those with global population size (PS) factor score of 5, 4, 3 or 2. Populations at PS = 2 are included if they are at the lower end of the range in this category (i.e., 69,200) and experiencing steep declines.

THE *BIRDS OF CONSERVATION CONCERN 2008* LISTS

To maximize the usefulness of this report to multiple partners, the *BCC 2008* lists are presented in 46 separate tables, comprising 37 BCR lists (Tables 2 to 38), 8 USFWS Region lists (Tables 39 to 47) and 1 National list (Table 48). Summaries of the status of each species at each of the three distinct geographic scales are provided in Appendix B, and a list of scientific names of all species mentioned is found in Appendix C. The BCR lists range from 10 to 53 species, USFWS Region lists range from 27 to 78 species, and the National list consists of 147 species. The number of priority species represents roughly 10 to 15 percent of all bird species of any given geographic unit.

BCR Lists

The number of species on individual BCR lists (Tables 2 to 38) ranges from 10 to 53, averaging about 27. Lists are generally larger for BCRs in the southern United States, reflecting greater species diversity at lower latitudes and the importance of these regions for wintering migrants. Island birds are at increased risk of becoming endangered. Thus, the "Other U.S. Pacific Islands" BCR and "U.S. Caribbean Islands" BCR have relatively high proportions of their native species represented as birds of conservation concern. Roughly ten percent of the bird species native to Hawaii (BCR 67) are identified as birds of conservation concern, but that region also has a disproportionately large number of bird species listed as either endangered or threatened under the ESA; combining birds of conservation concern with endangered or threatened species, about 25 percent of the native Hawaiian avifauna is at risk.

USFWS Region Lists

The number of species on individual USFWS Region lists (Tables 39 to 47) ranges from 27 to 78, averaging about 50. Following the trend seen in BCRs, USFWS Region lists of priority species are larger in the southern United States, although this is partially attributed by the disparities in area covered by each of the Regions. The birds on the USFWS Region lists generally represent about 10 percent of the species native to the respective Regions.

National List

The National list (Table 48) is comprised of 147 species, and includes disproportionately larger numbers of species from the orders Procellariformes (albatrosses, petrels, shearwaters, and storm-petrels), Charadriiformes (shorebirds, gulls, terns, and auks), and Piciformes (woodpeckers). Within the Charadriiformes, the families Charadriidae (plovers), Haematopodidae (oystercatchers), Scolopacidae (sandpipers), and Alcidae (murres, murrelets, and auklets) are represented on the list by greater numbers of species than expected. Among the Passeriformes—a large and diverse order of perching birds—the families Parulidae (wood-warblers) and Emberizidae (sparrows) and the subfamily Drepanidinae (Hawaiian honeycreepers) dominate the list in terms of both actual and relative numbers.

DISCUSSION

BCC 2008 is the latest update in a continuing effort to assess and prioritize bird species for conservation purposes (USFWS 1982, 1987, 1995, 2002; and U.S. Department of the Interior 1990). It is difficult to make meaningful comparisons among the lists because of differences in the way each succeeding report was prepared. In chronological order, these previous lists contained 28, 30, 77, 124, and 131 species of conservation concern at a National scale in 1982, 1987, 1990, 1995, and 2002 respectively; by comparison, *BCC 2008* includes 147 species at the National scale.

Do these figures reflect an actual decline in the conservation status of the Nation's birdlife, or do they merely reflect improvements in our ability to accurately identify and characterize species in real need of conservation attention? The truth probably lies somewhere in between. The preparation of prioritized species lists should be viewed as an evolving process, improving as our knowledge base increases, with each list reflecting the best available information at the time of its publication. The three bird conservation initiatives update their own assessments and scoring as new data or analyses become available. The data from these initiatives—which form the basis of *BCC 2008*—incorporate a great deal of input from many bird experts and have wide acceptance among members of avian conservation and scientific communities. We are confident that the methods used in *BCC 2008* are the best available for identifying avian conservation priorities as directed by the FWCA amendment of 1988.

Of the 131 species on the *BCC 2002* National list, 103 were retained on the current 2008 list and 28 were deleted due to a lack of convincing evidence that continued elevated concern is warranted. Forty-four species were added to the National list, resulting in a net gain of sixteen species for a current total of 147 species.

Of the 211 species on the Audubon WatchList (Butcher et al. 2007) that are not also a) endangered or threatened or b) hunted, 106 are on the *BCC 2008* National list and an additional 8 are on USFWS Region or BCR lists.

The selection criteria that we used identified 10 to 15 percent of all species at each geographic scale to be in need of additional conservation attention. Nongame migratory birds protected by the MBTA, the primary focus of this effort, make up an overwhelming proportion of the species on the *BCC 2008* lists. However, the proportional representation of non-MBTA species increases progressively at larger scales, reflecting the vulnerability of the island-endemic species that form the bulk of this group. The proportional representation of ESA candidate species also increases progressively at larger scales. ESA-delisted and ESA-proposed species make up a progressively smaller proportion of the species at larger scales.

BCC 2008 can be used as a barometer of the condition of our country's avifauna. Although there are general patterns that can be inferred from this report, there is no single reason why any species was placed on any one of these lists; some are relatively common but are undergoing sharp declines in population numbers, others are rare but may actually be increasing in numbers in certain locations, and others may be both rare and declining. However, habitat loss due to alteration or destruction continues to be the major reason for the declines of many species (Askins et al. 1990, USFWS 1995, Samson et al. 1998, Askins 2000). Birds included in the *BCC 2008* lists are deemed priorities for conservation actions, and the lists will be consulted for actions taken on Federal lands in accordance with Executive Order 13186, "Responsibilities of Federal agencies to protect migratory birds" (Clinton 2001). BCC species will also receive priority attention in the USFWS when allocating research, monitoring, and management funding. Our hope is that *BCC 2008* will stimulate coordinated, collaborative proactive conservation actions among Federal, State, and private partners.

LITERATURE CITED

Askins, R. A. 2000. Restoring North America's birds: lessons from landscape ecology. Yale University Press. 288 pp.

Askins, R. A., J. F. Lynch, and R. Greenberg. 1990. Population declines of migratory birds of eastern North America. Current Ornithology 7:1057-1077.

Bart, J., S. Brown, B. Harrington, and R. I. G. Morrison. 2007. Survey trends of North American shorebirds: population declines or shifting distributions? Journal of Avian Biology 38: 73–82.

Beissinger, S. R., J. M. Reed, J. M. Wunderle, Jr., S. K. Robinson, and D. M. Finch. 2000. Report of the AOU Conservation Committee on the Partners in Flight species prioritization plan. Auk 117:549-561.

Beissinger, S. R., E. C. Steadman, T. Wohlgenant, G. Blate, and S. Zack. 1996. Null models for assessing ecosystem conservation priorities: threatened birds as titers of threatened ecosystems. Conservation Biology 10:1343-1352.

Bradford, D. F., S. E. Franson, G. R. T. Miller, A. C. Neagle, G. E. Canterbury, and D. T. Heggem. 1998. Bird species assemblages as indicators of biotic integrity in Great Basin rangeland. Environmental Monitoring and Assessment 49:1-22.

Brown, S., C. Hickey, B. Gill, L. Gorman, C. Gratto-Trevor, S. Haig, B. Harrington, C. Hunter, G. Morrison, G. Page, P. Sanzenbacher, S. Skagen, N. Warnock. 2000. National shorebird conservation assessment: shorebird conservation status, conservation units, population estimates, population targets, and species prioritization. Manomet Center for Conservation Sciences, Manomet, Massachusetts. 54pp.
<http://www.fws.gov/shorebirdplan/USShorebird/PlanDocuments.htm>.

Brown, S., C. Hickey, B. Harrington, B., and R. Gill (eds.). 2001. The United States shorebird conservation plan. 2nd edition. Manomet Center for Conservation Sciences, Manomet, Massachusetts. 61 pp.
<http://www.fws.gov/shorebirdplan/USShorebird/downloads/USShorebirdPlan2Ed.pdf>.

Butcher, G.S., D.K. Niven, A.O. Panjabi, D.N. Pashley, and K.V. Rosenberg. WatchList: the 2007 WatchList for United States birds. American Birds 61:18-25.

Canterbury, G. E., T. E. Martin, D. R. Petit, L. J. Petit, and D. F. Bradford. 2000. Bird communities and habitat as ecological indicators of forest condition in regional monitoring. Conservation Biology 14:544-558.

Carter, M. F., W. C. Hunter, D. N. Pashley, and K. V. Rosenberg. 2000. Setting conservation priorities for landbirds in the United States: the Partners in Flight approach. Auk 117:541-548. <http://www.rmbo.org/pubs/downloads/pif.pdf>.

Central Intelligence Agency. 2001. The world factbook 2001. <http://www.cia.gov/cia/publications/factbook/index.html>.

Clinton, William J. 2001. Presidential Documents: Executive Order 13186 of January 10, 2001. Responsibilities of Federal agencies to protect migratory birds. Federal Register 66, No 11:3853-3856.

Dickinson, E.C. 2003. The Howard and Moore complete checklist of the birds of the world: third edition. Princeton University Press. 1056 pp.

Dunn, E. H. 1997. Setting priorities for conservation, research and monitoring of Canada's landbirds. Canadian Wildlife Service Technical Report 293.

Dunn, E. H., D. J. T. Hussell, and D. A. Welsh. 1999. Priority-setting tool applied to Canada's landbirds based on concern and responsibility for species. Conservation Biology 13:1404-1415.

Kushlan, J.A., M. J. Steinkamp, K. C. Parsons, J. Capp, M. A. Cruz, M. Coulter, I. Davidson, L. Dickson, N. Edelson, R. Elliot, and others. 2002. Waterbird Conservation for the Americas: the North American waterbird conservation plan, version 1. Waterbird Conservation for the Americas. Washington, DC.

Master, L. L. 1991. Assessing threats and setting priorities for conservation. Conservation Biology 5:559-563.

Millsap, B. A., J. A. Gore, D. E. Runde, and S. I. Cerulean. 1990. Setting priorities for the conservation of fish and wildlife species in Florida. Wildlife Monographs 111:1-57.

Morrison, R. I. G., B. J. McCaffery, R. E. Gill, S. K. Skagen, S. L. Jones, G. W. Page, C. L. Gratto-Trevor, and B. A. Andres. 2006. Population estimates of North American shorebirds, 2006. Wader Study Group Bulletin 111: 66–84.

O'Connell, T. J., L. E. Jackson, and R. P. Brooks. 2000. Bird guilds as indicators of ecological condition in the central Appalachians. Ecological Applications 10:1706-1721.

Panjabi, A. O., E. H. Dunn, P. J. Blancher, W. C. Hunter, B. Altman, J. Bart, C. J. Beardmore, H. Berlanga, G. S. Butcher, S. K. Davis, and others. 2005. The Partners in Flight handbook on species assessment. Version 2005. Partners in Flight Technical Series No. 3. <http://www.rmbo.org/pubs/downloads/Handbook2005.pdf>.

Rich, T. D., C. J. Beardmore, H. Berlanga, P. J. Blancher, M. S. W. Bradstreet, G. S. Butcher, D. W. Demarest, E. H. Dunn, W. C. Hunter, E. E. Iñigo-Elias, and others. 2004. Partners in Flight

North American Landbird Conservation Plan. Cornell Lab of Ornithology. Ithaca, NY. Partners in Flight website. < http://www.partnersinflight.org/cont_plan/>.

Samson, F. B., F. L. Knopf, and W. R. Ostlie. 1998. Grasslands. Pp. 437-472 in Status and trends of the nation's biological resources. Volume 2 (M. J. Mac et al., eds.). U.S. Department of the Interior, U.S. Geological Survey, Reston, Virginia. <http://biology.usgs.gov/stt/SNT/noframe/gr139.htm>.

U.S. Department of the Interior. 1990. Report of the Secretary of the Interior to the Congress of the United States on the federal conservation of migratory nongame birds pursuant to Section 13 of Public Law 96-366, the Fish and Wildlife Conservation Act of 1980, as revised. U.S. Fish and Wildlife Service, Washington, D.C. 61 pp.

U.S. Fish and Wildlife Service. 1982. Nongame migratory bird species with unstable or decreasing population trends in the United States. Office of Migratory Bird Management, Washington, D.C. 24 pp.

U.S. Fish and Wildlife Service. 1987. Migratory nongame birds of management concern in the United States: the 1987 list. Office of Migratory Bird Management, Washington, DC. 25 pp.

U.S. Fish and Wildlife Service. 1990. Conservation of avian diversity in North America. Office of Migratory Bird Management, Arlington, Virginia. 22 pp.

U.S. Fish and Wildlife Service. 1995. Migratory nongame birds of management concern in the United States: the 1995 List. Office of Migratory Bird Management, U.S. Fish and Wildlife Service, Arlington, Virginia. 22 pp.

U.S. Fish and Wildlife Service. 2002. Birds of conservation concern 2002. Division of Migratory Bird Management, Arlington, Virginia. 99 pp. <http://migratorybirds.fws.gov/reports/bcc2002.pdf>.

U.S. Fish and Wildlife Service. 2004. A blueprint for the future of migratory birds: Migratory Bird Program strategic plan 2004-2014. Division of Migratory Bird Management, U.S. Fish and Wildlife Service, Arlington, Virginia. 21 pp. <http://www.fws.gov/migratorybirds/mbstratplan/mbstratplan.htm>.

U.S. NABCI Committee. 2000a. North American Bird Conservation Initiative: bringing it all together. U.S. Fish and Wildlife Service, Arlington, Virginia. <http://www.nabci-us.org/aboutnabci/fwsbroch.pdf>.

U.S. NABCI Committee. 2000b. North American Bird Conservation Initiative Bird Conservation Regions map. U.S. Fish and Wildlife Service, Arlington, Virginia. <http://www.nabci-us.org/aboutnabci/map.pdf>

U.S. NABCI Committee. 2000c. Bird Conservation Region descriptions: a supplement to the North American Bird Conservation Initiative Bird Conservation Regions map. U.S. Fish and Wildlife Service, Arlington, Virginia. 38 pp. <http://www.nabci-us.org/aboutnabci/bcrdescrip.pdf>.

U.S. Shorebird Conservation Plan. 2004. High priority shorebirds — 2004. Unpublished Report, U. S. Fish and Wildlife Service, Arlington, Virginia. 5 pp. <http://www.fws.gov/shorebirdplan/USShorebird/downloads/ShorebirdPriorityPopulationsAug04.pdf >.

Venier, L. A., and J.L. Pearce. 2007. Boreal forest landbirds in relation to forest composition, structure, and landscape: implications for forest management. Canadian Journal of Forest Research-Revue Canadienne de Recherche Forestiere 37: 1214-1226.

Wilcove, D. S., D. Rothstein, J. Dubow, A. Phillips, and E. Losos. 1998. Quantifying threats to imperiled species in the United States. BioScience 48:607-615.

APPENDIX A

Figure 1   Map of the Bird Conservation Regions (BCRs) of the United States 3

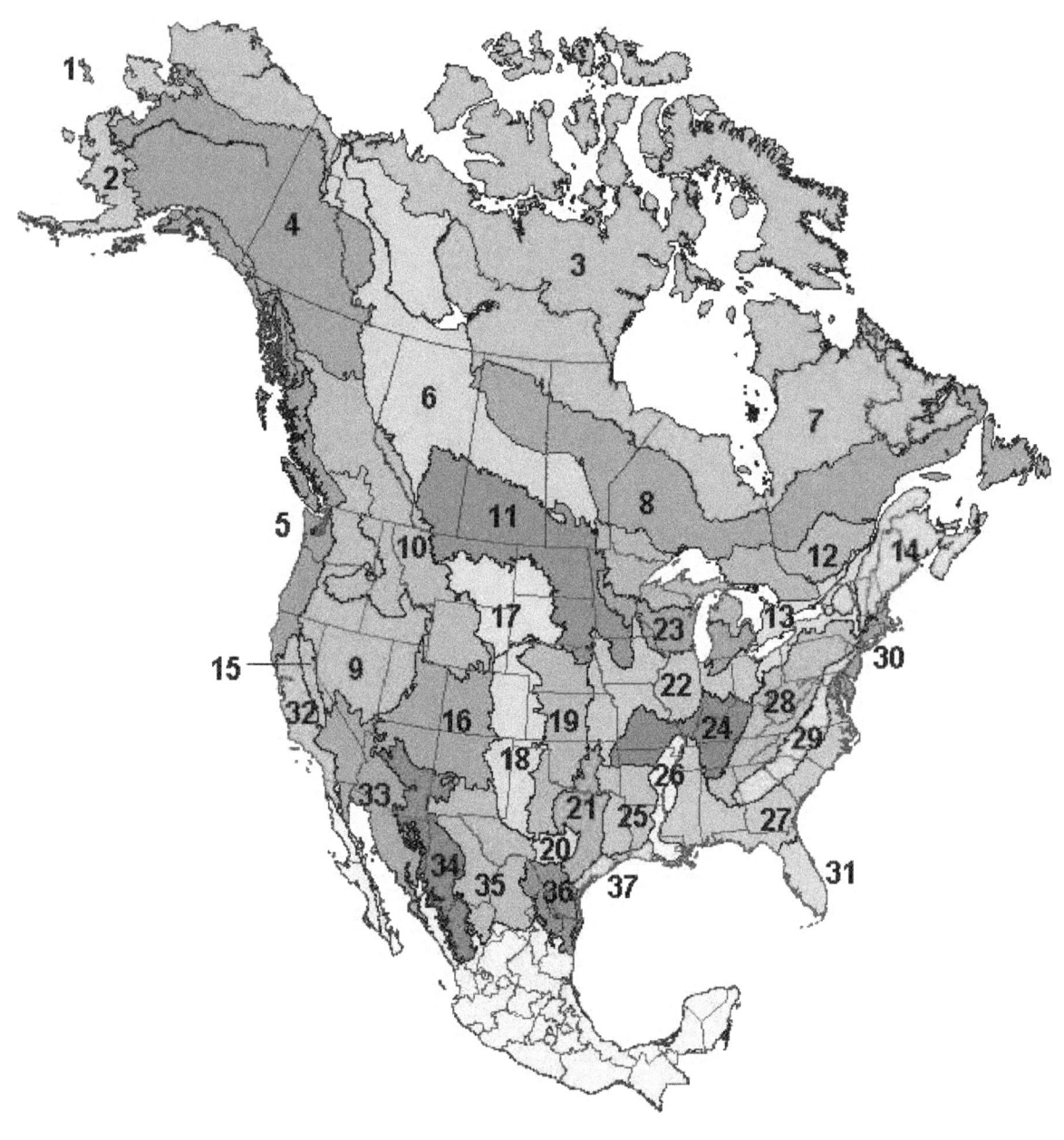

3 The figure does not show BCR 67 (Hawaii) or two other Bird Conservation Regions from the report that included islands in the Pacific and Caribbean which are either U.S. Territories or other affiliates.

Table 1 Eligibility of Various Species Groups for *BCC 2008* Consideration.

Applicable Federal Authority	Eligible	Not Eligible
Migratory Bird Treaty Act	"Nongame" and "other" species (as variously defined by bilateral migratory bird conventions with Canada, Mexico, Japan, and Russia)	Species peripheral to the U.S. (e.g., population fragments too small to be managed capably)
	"Gamebirds" (as defined by 50 CFR 20.11) for which hunting seasons have not recently been established (e.g., most shorebirds)	"Gamebirds" (as defined by 50 CFR 20.11) for which sport hunting seasons are established
	All subsistence-hunted species in Alaska (except "gamebirds" with established sport hunting seasons)	
Endangered Species Act	Candidates, including "resident gamebirds" (see below), or proposed Endangered or Threatened	Species, subspecies, and populations designated as Endangered or Threatened (as listed at 50 CFR 17.11)
	Non-listed subspecies and populations of otherwise Endangered or Threatened species (e.g., *occidentalis* ssp. of Spotted Owl)	
	Recently delisted MBTA species (e.g., Peregrine Falcon)	
	Other MBTA species delisted in the future	
None	Endemic Hawaiian honeycreepers of the subfamily Drepanididae (e.g., Hawai`i `Amakihi)	"Resident gamebirds" (generally hunted and managed by State wildlife agencies), unless listed as ESA Candidate (see above)
	Other island endemics (e.g., Fiji Shrikebill)	Non-native species

Table 2 BCR 1 (Aleutian/Bering Sea Islands) *BCC 2008* list[4]

Laysan Albatross (nb)
Black-footed Albatross (nb)
Red-faced Cormorant
Pelagic Cormorant
Black Oystercatcher
Rock Sandpiper (*ptilocnemis* ssp.)
Red-legged Kittiwake
Aleutian Tern
Arctic Tern
Marbled Murrelet (c)
Kittlitz's Murrelet (a)
Whiskered Auklet
McKay's Bunting

4 (a) ESA candidate, (b) ESA delisted, (c) non-listed subspecies or population of Threatened or Endangered species, (d) MBTA protection uncertain or lacking, (nb) non-breeding in this BCR

Table 3 BCR 2 (Western Alaska) *BCC 2008* list[5]

Red-throated Loon
Yellow-billed Loon
Red-faced Cormorant
Pelagic Cormorant
Peregrine Falcon (b)
Black Oystercatcher
Solitary Sandpiper
Lesser Yellowlegs
Whimbrel
Bristle-thighed Curlew
Hudsonian Godwit
Bar-tailed Godwit
Marbled Godwit
Red Knot (*roselaari* ssp.)
Rock Sandpiper (*ptilocnemis* ssp.) (nb)
Dunlin (*arcticola* ssp.) (nb)
Short-billed Dowitcher
Aleutian Tern
Arctic Tern
Marbled Murrelet (c)
Kittlitz's Murrelet (a)
McKay's Bunting (nb)

---

5 (a) ESA candidate, (b) ESA delisted, (c) non-listed subspecies or population of Threatened or Endangered species, (d) MBTA protection uncertain or lacking, (nb) non-breeding in this BCR

Table 4 BCR 3 (Arctic Plains and Mountains U.S. portion only) *BCC 2008* list.[6]

Red-throated Loon
Yellow-billed Loon
Peregrine Falcon (b)
Whimbrel
Bar-tailed Godwit
Red Knot (*roselaari* ssp.)
Dunlin (*arcticola* ssp.)
Buff-breasted Sandpiper
Arctic Tern
Smith's Longspur

---

6 (a) ESA candidate, (b) ESA delisted, (c) non-listed subspecies or population of Threatened or Endangered species, (d) MBTA protection uncertain or lacking, (nb) non-breeding in this BCR

Table 5 BCR 4 (Northwestern Interior Forest U.S. portion only) *BCC 2008* list.[7]

Horned Grebe
Peregrine Falcon (b)
Solitary Sandpiper
Lesser Yellowlegs
Upland Sandpiper
Whimbrel
Bristle-thighed Curlew
Hudsonian Godwit
Red Knot (*roselaari* ssp.)
Rock Sandpiper (*ptilocnemis* ssp.) (nb)
Short-billed Dowitcher
Olive-sided Flycatcher
Smith's Longspur
Rusty Blackbird

7 (a) ESA candidate, (b) ESA delisted, (c) non-listed subspecies or population of Threatened or Endangered species, (d) MBTA protection uncertain or lacking, (nb) non-breeding in this BCR

Table 6 BCR 5 (Northern Pacific Forest U.S. portions only) *BCC 2008* list.[8]

Yellow-billed Loon (nb)
Western Grebe (nb)
Laysan Albatross (nb)
Black-footed Albatross (nb)
Pink-footed Shearwater (nb)
Red-faced Cormorant
Pelagic Cormorant (*pelagicus* ssp.)
Bald Eagle (b)
Northern Goshawk (*laingi* ssp.)
Peregrine Falcon (b)
Black Oystercatcher
Solitary Sandpiper (nb)
Lesser Yellowlegs (nb)
Whimbrel (nb)
Long-billed Curlew (nb)
Hudsonian Godwit (nb)
Marbled Godwit (nb)
Red Knot (*roselaari* ssp.) (nb)
Short-billed Dowitcher (nb)
Aleutian Tern
Caspian Tern
Arctic Tern
Marbled Murrelet (c)
Kittlitz's Murrelet (a)
Black Swift
Rufous Hummingbird
Allen's Hummingbird
Olive-sided Flycatcher
Willow Flycatcher (c)
Horned Lark (*strigata* ssp.) (a)
Oregon Vesper Sparrow (*affinis* ssp.)
Purple Finch

---

8 (a) ESA candidate, (b) ESA delisted, (c) non-listed subspecies or population of Threatened or Endangered species, (d) MBTA protection uncertain or lacking, (nb) non-breeding in this BCR

Table 7 BCR 9 (Great Basin) *BCC 2008* list.[9]

Greater Sage-Grouse (Columbia Basin DPS) (a)
Eared Grebe (nb)
Bald Eagle (b)
Ferruginous Hawk
Golden Eagle
Peregrine Falcon (b)
Yellow Rail
Snowy Plover (c)
Long-billed Curlew
Marbled Godwit (nb)
Yellow-billed Cuckoo (w. U.S. DPS) (a)
Flammulated Owl
Black Swift
Calliope Hummingbird
Lewis's Woodpecker
Williamson's Sapsucker
White-headed Woodpecker
Willow Flycatcher (c)
Loggerhead Shrike
Pinyon Jay
Sage Thrasher
Virginia's Warbler
Green-tailed Towhee
Brewer's Sparrow
Black-chinned Sparrow
Sage Sparrow
Tricolored Blackbird
Black Rosy-Finch

---

9 (a) ESA candidate, (b) ESA delisted, (c) non-listed subspecies or population of Threatened or Endangered species, (d) MBTA protection uncertain or lacking, (nb) non-breeding in this BCR

Table 8 BCR 10 (Northern Rockies U.S. portion only) *BCC 2008* list.[10]

Bald Eagle (b)
Swainson's Hawk
Ferruginous Hawk
Peregrine Falcon (b)
Upland Sandpiper
Long-billed Curlew
Yellow-billed Cuckoo (w. U.S. DPS) (a)
Flammulated Owl
Black Swift
Calliope Hummingbird
Lewis's Woodpecker
Williamson's Sapsucker
White-headed Woodpecker
Olive-sided Flycatcher
Willow Flycatcher (c)
Loggerhead Shrike
Sage Thrasher
Brewer's Sparrow
Sage Sparrow
McCown's Longspur
Black Rosy-Finch
Cassin's Finch

---

10 (a) ESA candidate, (b) ESA delisted, (c) non-listed subspecies or population of Threatened or Endangered species, (d) MBTA protection uncertain or lacking, (nb) non-breeding in this BCR

Table 9 BCR 11 (Prairie Potholes U.S. portion only) *BCC 2008* list.[11]

Horned Grebe
American Bittern
Least Bittern
Bald Eagle (b)
Swainson's Hawk
Peregrine Falcon (b)
Yellow Rail
Mountain Plover
Solitary Sandpiper (nb)
Upland Sandpiper
Long-billed Curlew
Hudsonian Godwit (nb)
Marbled Godwit
Buff-breasted Sandpiper (nb)
Short-billed Dowitcher (nb)
Black Tern
Black-billed Cuckoo
Short-eared Owl
Red-headed Woodpecker
Sprague's Pipit
Grasshopper Sparrow
Baird's Sparrow
Nelson's Sharp-tailed Sparrow
McCown's Longspur
Smith's Longspur (nb)
Chestnut-collared Longspur
Dickcissel

11 (a) ESA candidate, (b) ESA delisted, (c) non-listed subspecies or population of Threatened or Endangered species, (d) MBTA protection uncertain or lacking, (nb) non-breeding in this BCR

Table 10 BCR 12 (Boreal Hardwood Transition U.S. portion only) *BCC 2008* list.[12]

Pied-billed Grebe
Horned Grebe (nb)
American Bittern
Bald Eagle (b)
Peregrine Falcon (b)
Yellow Rail
Solitary Sandpiper (nb)
Upland Sandpiper
Whimbrel (nb)
Hudsonian Godwit (nb)
Marbled Godwit (nb)
Red Knot (*rufa* ssp.) (a) (nb)
Buff-breasted Sandpiper (nb)
Short-billed Dowitcher (nb)
Black Tern
Common Tern
Red-headed Woodpecker
Olive-sided Flycatcher
Wood Thrush
Golden-winged Warbler
Canada Warbler
Henslow's Sparrow
Rusty Blackbird

---

12 (a) ESA candidate, (b) ESA delisted, (c) non-listed subspecies or population of Threatened or Endangered species, (d) MBTA protection uncertain or lacking, (nb) non-breeding in this BCR

Table 11 BCR 13 (Lower Great Lakes/St. Lawrence Plain U.S. portion only) *BCC 2008* list.[13]

Pied-billed Grebe
Horned Grebe (nb)
American Bittern
Least Bittern
Black-crowned Night-Heron
Bald Eagle (b)
Peregrine Falcon (b)
Solitary Sandpiper (nb)
Lesser Yellowlegs (nb)
Upland Sandpiper
Whimbrel (nb)
Hudsonian Godwit (nb)
Marbled Godwit (nb)
Red Knot (*rufa* ssp.) (a) (nb)
Semipalmated Sandpiper (Eastern) (nb)
Buff-breasted Sandpiper (nb)
Black Tern
Common Tern
Black-billed Cuckoo
Short-eared Owl (nb)
Red-headed Woodpecker
Wood Thrush
Blue-winged Warbler
Golden-winged Warbler
Cerulean Warbler
Canada Warbler
Henslow's Sparrow

13 (a) ESA candidate, (b) ESA delisted, (c) non-listed subspecies or population of Threatened or Endangered species, (d) MBTA protection uncertain or lacking, (nb) non-breeding in this BCR

Table 12 BCR 14 (Atlantic Northern Forests U.S. portion only) *BCC 2008* list.[14]

Red-throated Loon (nb)
Pied-billed Grebe
Horned Grebe (nb)
Greater Shearwater (nb)
Great Cormorant (nb)
American Bittern
Least Bittern
Snowy Egret
Bald Eagle (b)
Peregrine Falcon (b)
Yellow Rail
Solitary Sandpiper (nb)
Lesser Yellowlegs (nb)
Upland Sandpiper
Whimbrel (nb)
Hudsonian Godwit (nb)
Red Knot (*rufa* ssp.) (a) (nb)
Semipalmated Sandpiper (Eastern) (nb)
Purple Sandpiper (nb)
Arctic Tern
Olive-sided Flycatcher
Bicknell's Thrush
Wood Thrush
Blue-winged Warbler
Bay-breasted Warbler
Canada Warbler
Nelson's Sharp-tailed Sparrow
Saltmarsh Sharp-tailed Sparrow
Rusty Blackbird

---

14 (a) ESA candidate, (b) ESA delisted, (c) non-listed subspecies or population of Threatened or Endangered species, (d) MBTA protection uncertain or lacking, (nb) non-breeding in this BCR

Table 13 BCR 15 (Sierra Nevada) *BCC 2008* list.[15]

Bald Eagle (b)
Peregrine Falcon (b)
Flammulated Owl
Spotted Owl (*occidentalis* ssp.) (c)
Black Swift
Calliope Hummingbird
Lewis's Woodpecker
Williamson's Sapsucker
Olive-sided Flycatcher
Willow Flycatcher (c)
Cassin's Finch

---

15 (a) ESA candidate, (b) ESA delisted, (c) non-listed subspecies or population of Threatened or Endangered species, (d) MBTA protection uncertain or lacking, (nb) non-breeding in this BCR

Table 14 BCR 16 (Southern Rockies/Colorado Plateau) *BCC 2008* list.[16]

Gunnison Sage Grouse
American Bittern
Bald Eagle (b)
Ferruginous Hawk
Golden Eagle
Peregrine Falcon (b)
Prairie Falcon
Snowy Plover (c)
Mountain Plover
Long-billed Curlew
Yellow-billed Cuckoo (w. U.S. DPS) (a)
Flammulated Owl
Burrowing Owl
Lewis's Woodpecker
Willow Flycatcher (c)
Gray Vireo
Pinyon Jay
Juniper Titmouse
Veery
Bendire's Thrasher
Grace's Warbler
Brewer's Sparrow
Grasshopper Sparrow
Chestnut-collared Longspur
Black Rosy-Finch
Brown-capped Rosy-Finch
Cassin's Finch

16 (a) ESA candidate, (b) ESA delisted, (c) non-listed subspecies or population of Threatened or Endangered species, (d) MBTA protection uncertain or lacking, (nb) non-breeding in this BCR

Table 15 BCR 17 (Badlands and Prairies) *BCC 2008* list.[17]

Horned Grebe
American Bittern
Bald Eagle (b)
Ferruginous Hawk
Golden Eagle
Peregrine Falcon (b)
Prairie Falcon
Yellow Rail
Mountain Plover
Upland Sandpiper
Long-billed Curlew
Marbled Godwit
Black-billed Cuckoo
Burrowing Owl
Short-eared Owl
Lewis's Woodpecker
Red-headed Woodpecker
Loggerhead Shrike
Pinyon Jay
Sage Thrasher
Sprague's Pipit
Brewer's Sparrow
Sage Sparrow
Grasshopper Sparrow
Baird's Sparrow
McCown's Longspur
Chestnut-collared Longspur
Dickcissel

---

17 (a) ESA candidate, (b) ESA delisted, (c) non-listed subspecies or population of Threatened or Endangered species, (d) MBTA protection uncertain or lacking, (nb) non-breeding in this BCR

Table 16 BCR 18 (Shortgrass Prairie) *BCC 2008* list.[18]

Lesser Prairie-Chicken (a)
Bald Eagle (b)
Golden Eagle
Prairie Falcon
Snowy Plover (c)
Mountain Plover
Upland Sandpiper
Long-billed Curlew
Burrowing Owl
Lewis's Woodpecker
Willow Flycatcher (c)
Bell's Vireo (c)
Sprague's Pipit (nb)
Lark Bunting
McCown's Longspur
Chestnut-collared Longspur

---

18 (a) ESA candidate, (b) ESA delisted, (c) non-listed subspecies or population of Threatened or Endangered species, (d) MBTA protection uncertain or lacking, (nb) non-breeding in this BCR

Table 17 BCR 19 (Central Mixed-Grass Prairie) *BCC 2008* list.[19]

Lesser Prairie-Chicken (a)
Little Blue Heron
Mississippi Kite
Bald Eagle (b)
Swainson's Hawk
Black Rail
Snowy Plover (c)
Mountain Plover (nb)
Solitary Sandpiper (nb)
Upland Sandpiper
Long-billed Curlew
Hudsonian Godwit (nb)
Marbled Godwit (nb)
Buff-breasted Sandpiper (nb)
Short-billed Dowitcher (nb)
Red-headed Woodpecker
Scissor-tailed Flycatcher
Loggerhead Shrike
Bell's Vireo (c)
Sprague's Pipit (nb)
Cassin's Sparrow
Lark Bunting
Henslow's Sparrow
Harris's Sparrow (nb)
McCown's Longspur (nb)
Smith's Longspur (nb)
Chestnut-collared Longspur (nb)

---

19 (a) ESA candidate, (b) ESA delisted, (c) non-listed subspecies or population of Threatened or Endangered species, (d) MBTA protection uncertain or lacking, (nb) non-breeding in this BCR

Table 18 BCR 20 (Edwards Plateau) *BCC 2008* list.[20]

Bald Eagle (b)
Peregrine Falcon (b)
Mountain Plover (nb)
Upland Sandpiper (nb)
Long-billed Curlew (nb)
Gray Vireo
Rufous-crowned Sparrow
Harris's Sparrow (nb)
McCown's Longspur (nb)
Chestnut-collared Longspur (nb)
Orchard Oriole

---

20 (a) ESA candidate, (b) ESA delisted, (c) non-listed subspecies or population of Threatened or Endangered species, (d) MBTA protection uncertain or lacking, (nb) non-breeding in this BCR

Table 19 BCR 21 (Oaks and Prairies) *BCC 2008* list.[21]

Little Blue Heron
Swallow-tailed Kite
Bald Eagle (b)
Peregrine Falcon (b)
Black Rail (nb)
Upland Sandpiper
Long-billed Curlew (nb)
Hudsonian Godwit (nb)
Buff-breasted Sandpiper (nb)
Red-headed Woodpecker
Scissor-tailed Flycatcher
Loggerhead Shrike
Bell's Vireo (c)
Sprague's Pipit (nb)
Swainson's Warbler
Henslow's Sparrow (nb)
Harris's Sparrow (nb)
Smith's Longspur (nb)
Orchard Oriole

---

21 (a) ESA candidate, (b) ESA delisted, (c) non-listed subspecies or population of Threatened or Endangered species, (d) MBTA protection uncertain or lacking, (nb) non-breeding in this BCR

Table 20 BCR 22 (Eastern Tallgrass Prairie) *BCC 2008* list.[22]

Pied-billed Grebe
Horned Grebe (nb)
American Bittern
Least Bittern
Black-crowned Night-Heron
Bald Eagle (b)
Peregrine Falcon (b)
Black Rail
Solitary Sandpiper (nb)
Upland Sandpiper
Whimbrel (nb)
Hudsonian Godwit (nb)
Marbled Godwit (nb)
Red Knot (*roselaari* ssp.) (nb)
Red Knot (*rufa* ssp.) (a) (nb)
Buff-breasted Sandpiper (nb)
Short-billed Dowitcher (nb)
Black Tern
Common Tern
Black-billed Cuckoo
Short-eared Owl (nb)
Whip-poor-will
Red-headed Woodpecker
Northern Flicker
Acadian Flycatcher
Loggerhead Shrike
Bell's Vireo (c)
Bewick's Wren (*bewickii* ssp.)
Wood Thrush
Blue-winged Warbler
Cerulean Warbler
Prothonotary Warbler
Kentucky Warbler
Field Sparrow
Grasshopper Sparrow
Henslow's Sparrow
Smith's Longspur (nb)

Dickcissel
Rusty Blackbird (nb)

22 (a) ESA candidate, (b) ESA delisted, (c) non-listed subspecies or population of Threatened or Endangered species, (d) MBTA protection uncertain or lacking, (nb) non-breeding in this BCR

Table 21 BCR 23 (Prairie Hardwood Transition) *BCC 2008* list.[23]

Pied-billed Grebe
Horned Grebe (nb)
American Bittern
Bald Eagle (b)
Peregrine Falcon (b)
Yellow Rail
Solitary Sandpiper (nb)
Upland Sandpiper
Whimbrel (nb)
Hudsonian Godwit (nb)
Marbled Godwit (nb)
Red Knot (*roselaar*i ssp.) (nb)
Red Knot (*rufa* ssp.) (a) (nb)
Buff-breasted Sandpiper (nb)
Short-billed Dowitcher (nb)
Black Tern
Common Tern
Black-billed Cuckoo
Short-eared Owl (nb)
Red-headed Woodpecker
Willow Flycatcher (c)
Marsh Wren
Brown Thrasher
Blue-winged Warbler
Golden-winged Warbler
Cerulean Warbler
Henslow's Sparrow
Dickcissel
Bobolink
Rusty Blackbird (nb)

---

23 (a) ESA candidate, (b) ESA delisted, (c) non-listed subspecies or population of Threatened or Endangered species, (d) MBTA protection uncertain or lacking, (nb) non-breeding in this BCR

Table 22 BCR 24 (Central Hardwoods) *BCC 2008* list.[24]

Bald Eagle (b)
Peregrine Falcon (b)
Black Rail
Solitary Sandpiper (nb)
Buff-breasted Sandpiper (nb)
Short-eared Owl (nb)
Whip-poor-will
Red-headed Woodpecker
Loggerhead Shrike
Bell's Vireo (c)
Brown-headed Nuthatch
Bewick's Wren (*bewickii* ssp.)
Sedge Wren
Wood Thrush
Blue-winged Warbler
Prairie Warbler
Cerulean Warbler
Worm-eating Warbler
Swainson's Warbler
Kentucky Warbler
Bachman's Sparrow
Henslow's Sparrow
LeConte's Sparrow (nb)
Smith's Longspur (nb)
Painted Bunting
Rusty Blackbird (nb)

---

24 (a) ESA candidate, (b) ESA delisted, (c) non-listed subspecies or population of Threatened or Endangered species, (d) MBTA protection uncertain or lacking, (nb) non-breeding in this BCR

Table 23 BCR 25 (West Gulf Coastal Plain/Ouachitas) *BCC 2008* list.[25]

Least Bittern
Little Blue Heron
Swallow-tailed Kite
Bald Eagle (b)
American Kestrel (*paulus* ssp.)
Yellow Rail (nb)
Solitary Sandpiper (nb)
Hudsonian Godwit (nb)
Buff-breasted Sandpiper (nb)
Chuck-will's-widow
Red-headed Woodpecker
Loggerhead Shrike
Brown-headed Nuthatch
Bewick's Wren (*bewickii* ssp.)
Wood Thrush
Sprague's Pipit (nb)
Prairie Warbler
Cerulean Warbler
Prothonotary Warbler
Worm-eating Warbler
Swainson's Warbler
Louisiana Waterthrush
Kentucky Warbler
Bachman's Sparrow
Henslow's Sparrow (nb)
Smith's Longspur (nb)
Painted Bunting
Orchard Oriole

---

25 (a) ESA candidate, (b) ESA delisted, (c) non-listed subspecies or population of Threatened or Endangered species, (d) MBTA protection uncertain or lacking, (nb) non-breeding in this BCR

Table 24 BCR 26 (Mississippi Alluvial Valley) *BCC 2008* list.[26]

American Bittern (nb)
Least Bittern
Swallow-tailed Kite
Bald Eagle (b)
Peregrine Falcon (b)
Yellow Rail (nb)
Black Rail
Solitary Sandpiper (nb)
Hudsonian Godwit (nb)
Marbled Godwit (nb)
Buff-breasted Sandpiper (nb)
Short-billed Dowitcher (nb)
Short-eared Owl (nb)
Red-headed Woodpecker
Sedge Wren (nb)
Wood Thrush
Cerulean Warbler
Prothonotary Warbler
Swainson's Warbler
Kentucky Warbler
Henslow's Sparrow (nb)
LeConte's Sparrow (nb)
Painted Bunting
Dickcissel
Rusty Blackbird (nb)
Orchard Oriole

---

26 (a) ESA candidate, (b) ESA delisted, (c) non-listed subspecies or population of Threatened or Endangered species, (d) MBTA protection uncertain or lacking, (nb) non-breeding in this BCR

Table 25 BCR 27 (Southeastern Coastal Plain) *BCC 2008* list.[27]

Red-throated Loon
Black-capped Petrel (nb)
Audubon's Shearwater (nb)
American Bittern (nb)
Least Bittern
Roseate Spoonbill (nb)
Swallow-tailed Kite
Bald Eagle (b)
American Kestrel (*paulus* ssp.)
Peregrine Falcon (b)
Yellow Rail (nb)
Black Rail
Limpkin
Snowy Plover (c)
Wilson's Plover
American Oystercatcher
Solitary Sandpiper (nb)
Upland Sandpiper (nb)
Whimbrel (nb)
Long-billed Curlew (nb)
Marbled Godwit (nb)
Red Knot (*rufa* ssp.) (a) (nb)
Semipalmated Sandpiper (Eastern) (nb)
Buff-breasted Sandpiper (nb)
Short-billed Dowitcher (nb)
Least Tern (c)
Gull-billed Tern

Sandwich Tern
Black Skimmer
Common Ground-Dove
Chuck-will's-widow
Whip-poor-will
Red-headed Woodpecker
Loggerhead Shrike
Brown-headed Nuthatch
Bewick's Wren (*bewickii* ssp.)
Sedge Wren (nb)
Wood Thrush
Blue-winged Warbler
Black-throated Green Warbler
Prairie Warbler
Cerulean Warbler
Prothonotary Warbler
Swainson's Warbler
Kentucky Warbler
Bachman's Sparrow
Henslow's Sparrow
LeConte's Sparrow (nb)
Nelson's Sharp-tailed Sparrow (nb)
Saltmarsh Sharp-tailed Sparrow (nb)
Seaside Sparrow (c)
Painted Bunting
Rusty Blackbird (nb)

---

27 (a) ESA candidate, (b) ESA delisted, (c) non-listed subspecies or population of Threatened or Endangered species, (d) MBTA protection uncertain or lacking, (nb) non-breeding in this BCR

Table 26 BCR 28 (Appalachian Mountains) *BCC 2008* list.[28]

Bald Eagle (b)
Peregrine Falcon (b)
Upland Sandpiper
Northern Saw-whet Owl (S. Appalachian breeding pop.)
Whip-poor-will
Red-headed Woodpecker
Yellow-bellied Sapsucker (S. Appalachian breeding pop.)
Olive-sided Flycatcher
Loggerhead Shrike
Black-capped Chickadee (S. Appalachian pop.)
Bewick's Wren (*bewickii* ssp.)
Sedge Wren (nb)
Wood Thrush
Blue-winged Warbler
Golden-winged Warbler
Prairie Warbler
Cerulean Warbler
Worm-eating Warbler
Swainson's Warbler
Louisiana Waterthrush
Kentucky Warbler
Canada Warbler
Henslow's Sparrow
Rusty Blackbird (nb)
Red Crossbill (S. Appalachian pop.)

---

28 (a) ESA candidate, (b) ESA delisted, (c) non-listed subspecies or population of Threatened or Endangered species, (d) MBTA protection uncertain or lacking, (nb) non-breeding in this BCR

Table 27 BCR 29 (Piedmont) *BCC 2008* list.[29]

Bald Eagle (b)
Peregrine Falcon (b)
Black Rail
Short-eared Owl (nb)
Whip-poor-will
Loggerhead Shrike
Brown-headed Nuthatch
Bewick's Wren (*bewickii* ssp.)
Sedge Wren
Wood Thrush
Blue-winged Warbler
Prairie Warbler
Cerulean Warbler
Swainson's Warbler
Kentucky Warbler
Bachman's Sparrow
Henslow's Sparrow
Rusty Blackbird (nb)

29 (a) ESA candidate, (b) ESA delisted, (c) non-listed subspecies or population of Threatened or Endangered species, (d) MBTA protection uncertain or lacking, (nb) non-breeding in this BCR

Table 28 BCR 30 (New England/Mid-Atlantic Coast) *BCC 2008* list.[30]

Red-throated Loon (nb)
Pied-billed Grebe
Horned Grebe (nb)
Greater Shearwater (nb)
Audubon's Shearwater (nb)
American Bittern
Least Bittern
Snowy Egret
Bald Eagle (b)
Peregrine Falcon (b)
Black Rail
Wilson's Plover
American Oystercatcher
Solitary Sandpiper (nb)
Lesser Yellowlegs (nb)
Upland Sandpiper
Whimbrel (nb)
Hudsonian Godwit (nb)
Marbled Godwit (nb)
Red Knot (*rufa* ssp.) (a) (nb)
Semipalmated Sandpiper (Eastern) (nb)
Purple Sandpiper (nb)
Buff-breasted Sandpiper (nb)

Short-billed Dowitcher (nb)
Least Tern (c)
Gull-billed Tern
Black Skimmer
Short-eared Owl (nb)
Whip-poor-will
Red-headed Woodpecker
Loggerhead Shrike
Brown-headed Nuthatch
Sedge Wren
Wood Thrush
Blue-winged Warbler
Golden-winged Warbler
Prairie Warbler
Cerulean Warbler
Worm-eating Warbler
Kentucky Warbler
Henslow's Sparrow
Nelson's Sharp-tailed Sparrow
Saltmarsh Sharp-tailed Sparrow
Seaside Sparrow (c)
Rusty Blackbird (nb)

---

30 (a) ESA candidate, (b) ESA delisted, (c) non-listed subspecies or population of Threatened or Endangered species, (d) MBTA protection uncertain or lacking, (nb) non-breeding in this BCR

Table 29 BCR 31 (Peninsular Florida) *BCC 2008* list.[31]

Black-capped Petrel (nb)
Audubon's Shearwater (nb)
Brown Booby (nb)
Magnificent Frigatebird
American Bittern (nb)
Least Bittern
Reddish Egret
Roseate Spoonbill
Swallow-tailed Kite
Bald Eagle (b)
Short-tailed Hawk
American Kestrel (*paulus* ssp.)
Peregrine Falcon (b)
Yellow Rail (nb)
Black Rail
Limpkin
Snowy Plover (c)
Wilson's Plover
American Oystercatcher
Solitary Sandpiper (nb)
Lesser Yellowlegs (nb)
Whimbrel (nb)
Long-billed Curlew (nb)
Marbled Godwit (nb)
Red Knot (*rufa* ssp.) (a) (nb)

Semipalmated Sandpiper (Eastern) (nb)
Buff-breasted Sandpiper (nb)
Short-billed Dowitcher (nb)
Least Tern (c)
Black Skimmer
White-crowned Pigeon
Common Ground-Dove
Mangrove Cuckoo
Smooth-billed Ani
Chuck-will's-widow
Red-headed Woodpecker
Loggerhead Shrike
Black-whiskered Vireo
Brown-headed Nuthatch
Yellow Warbler (*gundlachi* ssp.)
Prairie Warbler
Prothonotary Warbler
Bachman's Sparrow
Grasshopper Sparrow
Henslow's Sparrow (nb)
Nelson's Sharp-tailed Sparrow (nb)
Saltmarsh Sharp-tailed Sparrow (nb)
Seaside Sparrow (c)
Painted Bunting (nb)

---

31 (a) ESA candidate, (b) ESA delisted, (c) non-listed subspecies or population of Threatened or Endangered species, (d) MBTA protection uncertain or lacking, (nb) non-breeding in this BCR

Table 30 BCR 32 (Coastal California U.S. portion only) *BCC 2008* list.[32]

Black-footed Albatross (nb)
Pink-footed Shearwater (nb)
Black-vented Shearwater (nb)
Ashy Storm-Petrel
Bald Eagle (b)
Peregrine Falcon (b)
Yellow Rail (nb)
Black Rail
Snowy Plover (c)
Mountain Plover (nb)
Black Oystercatcher
Whimbrel (nb)
Long-billed Curlew (nb)
Marbled Godwit (nb)
Red Knot (*roselaari* ssp.) (nb)
Short-billed Dowitcher (nb)
Gull-billed Tern
Black Skimmer
Xantus's Murrelet (a)
Cassin's Auklet
Yellow-billed Cuckoo (w. US DPS) (a)
Flammulated Owl
Burrowing Owl

Spotted Owl (*occidentalis* ssp.) (c)
Black Swift
Costa's Hummingbird
Allen's Hummingbird
Lewis's Woodpecker
Nuttall's Woodpecker
White-headed Woodpecker
Loggerhead Shrike
Island Scrub-Jay
Yellow-billed Magpie
Oak Titmouse
Cactus Wren
LeConte's Thrasher
Yellow Warbler (*brewsteri* ssp.)
Common Yellowthroat (*sinuosa* ssp.)
Spotted Towhee (*clementae* ssp.)
Black-chinned Sparrow
Song Sparrow (*graminea* ssp.)
Song Sparrow (*maxillaris* ssp.)
Song Sparrow (*pusillula* ssp.)
Song Sparrow (*samuelis* ssp.)
Tricolored Blackbird
Lawrence's Goldfinch

---

32 (a) ESA candidate, (b) ESA delisted, (c) non-listed subspecies or population of Threatened or Endangered species, (d) MBTA protection uncertain or lacking, (nb) non-breeding in this BCR

Table 31 BCR 33 (Sonoran and Mojave Deserts U.S. portion only) *BCC 2008* list.[33]

Least Bittern
Bald Eagle (b)
Peregrine Falcon (b)
Prairie Falcon
Black Rail
Snowy Plover (c)
Mountain Plover (nb)
Whimbrel (nb)
Long-billed Curlew (nb)
Marbled Godwit (nb)
Red Knot (*roselaari* ssp.) (nb)
Gull-billed Tern
Black Skimmer
Yellow-billed Cuckoo (w. US DPS) (a)
Elf Owl
Burrowing Owl
Costa's Hummingbird
Gila Woodpecker
Gilded Flicker
Bell's Vireo (c)
Gray Vireo
Bendire's Thrasher
LeConte's Thrasher
Lucy's Warbler
Yellow Warbler (*sonorana* ssp.)
Rufous-winged Sparrow
Black-chinned Sparrow
Lawrence's Goldfinch

33 (a) ESA candidate, (b) ESA delisted, (c) non-listed subspecies or population of Threatened or Endangered species, (d) MBTA protection uncertain or lacking, (nb) non-breeding in this BCR

Table 32 BCR 34 (Sierra Madre Occidental U.S. portion only) *BCC 2008* list.[34]

Bald Eagle (b)
Common Black-Hawk
Peregrine Falcon (b)
Mountain Plover (nb)
Yellow-billed Cuckoo (w. U.S. DPS) (a)
Flammulated Owl
Elf Owl
Blue-throated Hummingbird
Elegant Trogon
Lewis's Woodpecker
Arizona Woodpecker
Northern Beardless-Tyrannulet
Buff-breasted Flycatcher
Rose-throated Becard
Bell's Vireo (c)
Gray Vireo
Pinyon Jay
Bendire's Thrasher
Sprague's Pipit (nb)
Phainopepla
Olive Warbler
Lucy's Warbler
Yellow Warbler (*sonorana* ssp.)
Black-throated Gray Warbler
Grace's Warbler
Red-faced Warbler
Canyon Towhee
Rufous-winged Sparrow
Botteri's Sparrow
Five-striped Sparrow
Black-chinned Sparrow
Lark Bunting (nb)
Grasshopper Sparrow (nb)
Grasshopper Sparrow (*ammolegus* ssp.)
Baird's Sparrow (nb)
Chestnut-collared Longspur (nb)
Varied Bunting

---

34 (a) ESA candidate, (b) ESA delisted, (c) non-listed subspecies or population of Threatened or Endangered species, (d) MBTA protection uncertain or lacking, (nb) non-breeding in this BCR

Table 33 BCR 35 (Chihuahuan Desert U.S. portion only) *BCC 2008* lists.[35]

Bald Eagle (b)
Common Black-Hawk
Ferruginous Hawk (nb)
Golden Eagle
Peregrine Falcon (b)
Snowy Plover (c)
Mountain Plover
Long-billed Curlew (nb)
Yellow-billed Cuckoo (w. US DPS) (a)
Flammulated Owl
Elf Owl
Burrowing Owl
Lucifer Hummingbird
Loggerhead Shrike
Bell's Vireo (c)
Gray Vireo
Bendire's Thrasher
Sprague's Pipit (nb)
Virginia's Warbler
Colima Warbler
Yellow Warbler (*sonorana* ssp.)
Grace's Warbler
Red-faced Warbler
Cassin's Sparrow
Black-chinned Sparrow
Lark Bunting (nb)
Baird's Sparrow (nb)
McCown's Longspur (nb)
Chestnut-collared Longspur (nb)
Varied Bunting
Painted Bunting

---

35 (a) ESA candidate, (b) ESA delisted, (c) non-listed subspecies or population of Threatened or Endangered species, (d) MBTA protection uncertain or lacking, (nb) non-breeding in this BCR

Table 34 BCR 36 (Tamaulipan Brushlands U.S. portion only) *BCC 2008* list.[36]

Harris's Hawk
Swainson's Hawk
Snowy Plover (c)
Mountain Plover (nb)
Solitary Sandpiper (nb)
Lesser Yellowlegs (nb)
Long-billed Curlew (nb)
Gull-billed Tern
Red-billed Pigeon
Green Parakeet (d)
Red-crowned Parrot (d)
Elf Owl
Burrowing Owl
Buff-bellied Hummingbird
Northern Beardless-Tyrannulet
Rose-throated Becard
Bell's Vireo (c)
Verdin
Curve-billed Thrasher
Sprague's Pipit (nb)
Tropical Parula
Summer Tanager
White-collared Seedeater
Cassin's Sparrow
Lark Bunting (nb)
Chestnut-collared Longspur (nb)
Varied Bunting
Painted Bunting
Dickcissel
Hooded Oriole
Altamira Oriole
Audubon's Oriole

---

36 (a) ESA candidate, (b) ESA delisted, (c) non-listed subspecies or population of Threatened or Endangered species, (d) MBTA protection uncertain or lacking, (nb) non-breeding in this BCR

Table 35 BCR 37 (Gulf Coastal Prairie U.S. portion only) *BCC 2008* list.[37]

Audubon's Shearwater (nb)
Band-rumped Storm-Petrel (nb)
American Bittern
Least Bittern
Reddish Egret
Swallow-tailed Kite
Bald Eagle (b)
White-tailed Hawk
Peregrine Falcon (b) (nb)
Yellow Rail (nb)
Black Rail
Snowy Plover (c)
Wilson's Plover
Mountain Plover (nb)
American Oystercatcher
Solitary Sandpiper (nb)
Lesser Yellowlegs (nb)
Upland Sandpiper (nb)
Whimbrel (nb)
Long-billed Curlew
Hudsonian Godwit (nb)
Marbled Godwit (nb)
Red Knot (*roselaari* ssp.) (nb)

Red Knot (*rufa* ssp.) (a) (nb)
Buff-breasted Sandpiper (nb)
Short-billed Dowitcher (nb)
Least Tern (c)
Gull-billed Tern
Sandwich Tern
Black Skimmer
Short-eared Owl (nb)
Loggerhead Shrike
Sedge Wren (nb)
Sprague's Pipit (nb)
Prothonotary Warbler
Swainson's Warbler
Botteri's Sparrow
Grasshopper Sparrow
Henslow's Sparrow (nb)
LeConte's Sparrow (nb)
Nelson's Sharp-tailed Sparrow (nb)
Seaside Sparrow (c)
Painted Bunting
Dickcissel

---

37 (a) ESA candidate, (b) ESA delisted, (c) non-listed subspecies or population of Threatened or Endangered species, (d) MBTA protection uncertain or lacking, (nb) non-breeding in this BCR

Table 36 BCR 67 (Hawaii) *BCC 2008* list.[38]

Laysan Albatross
Black-footed Albatross
Christmas Shearwater
Band-rumped Storm-Petrel (a)
Tristram's Storm-Petrel
Bristle-thighed Curlew (nb)
Short-eared Owl
`Elepaio (d)
`Oma`o
Hawai`i `Amakihi (d)
Oahu `Amakihi (d)
Kaua`i `Amakihi (d)
`Anianiau (d)
`Akikiki (a,d)
Maui `Alauahio (d)
`Akeke`e (d)
`I`iwi (d)
`Apapane (d)

---

38 (a) ESA candidate, (b) ESA delisted, (c) non-listed subspecies or population of Threatened or Endangered species, (d) MBTA protection uncertain or lacking, (nb) non-breeding in this BCR

Table 37 Other U.S. Pacific Islands *BCC 2008* list.[39]

Laysan Albatross
Black-footed Albatross
Herald Petrel
Tahiti Petrel (d)
Phoenix Petrel (d)
Christmas Shearwater
Audubon's Shearwater
Polynesian Storm-Petrel (d)
Spotless Crake (American Samoa pop.) (a,d)
Purple Swamphen
Bristle-thighed Curlew (nb)
Friendly Ground-Dove (American Samoa DPS) (a,d)
Micronesian Myzomela (d)
Rufous Fantail (*mariae* ssp.) (d)
Rufous Fantail (*saipanensis* ssp.) (d)
Fiji Shrikebill (d)
Tinian Monarch (d)
Bridled White-eye (*saypani* ssp.) (c,d)
Golden White-eye (d)
Micronesian Starling (*guami* ssp.) (d)
Polynesian Starling (d)

---

39 (a) ESA candidate, (b) ESA delisted, (c) non-listed subspecies or population of Threatened or Endangered species, (d) MBTA protection uncertain or lacking, (nb) non-breeding in this BCR

Table 38 U.S. Caribbean Islands (Puerto Rico and U.S. Virgin Islands) *BCC 2008* list.[40]

West Indian Whistling-Duck
White-cheeked Pintail
Masked Duck
Ruddy Duck (*jamaicensis* ssp.)
Audubon's Shearwater
Masked Booby
Brown Booby
Red-footed Booby
Magnificent Frigatebird
Least Bittern
American Flamingo
Black Rail
Yellow-breasted Crake
Caribbean Coot
Limpkin
Snowy Plover (c)
Wilson's Plover
American Oystercatcher
Red Knot (*rufa* ssp.) (a) (nb)
Semipalmated Sandpiper (Eastern) (nb)
White-crowned Pigeon
Bridled Quail-Dove
Antillean Mango (d)
Loggerhead Kingbird
Puerto Rican Vireo
Elfin-woods Warbler (a)
Greater Antillean Oriole

---

40 (a) ESA candidate, (b) ESA delisted, (c) non-listed subspecies or population of Threatened or Endangered species, (d) MBTA protection uncertain or lacking, (nb) non-breeding in this BCR

Table 39 USFWS Region 1 (Pacific Region) *BCC 2008* list.[41]

Greater Sage-Grouse (Columbia Basin DPS)(a)
Black-footed Albatross
Herald Petrel
Tahiti Petrel (d)
Phoenix Petrel (d)
Pink-footed Shearwater (nb)
Polynesian Storm-Petrel (d)
Band-rumped Storm-Petrel (a)
Tristram's Storm-Petrel
Bald Eagle (b)
Swainson's Hawk
Ferruginous Hawk
Peregrine Falcon (b)
Yellow Rail
Spotless Crake (American Samoa pop.) (a,d)
Purple Swamphen
Snowy Plover (c)
Black Oystercatcher
Whimbrel (nb)
Bristle-thighed Curlew (nb)
Long-billed Curlew
Marbled Godwit (nb)
Red Knot (*roselaari* ssp.) (nb)
Short-billed Dowitcher (nb)
Friendly Ground-Dove (American Samoa DPS) (a,d)
Yellow-billed Cuckoo (w. US DPS) (a)
Flammulated Owl
Short-eared Owl
Black Swift
Calliope Hummingbird

Rufous Hummingbird
Lewis's Woodpecker
Williamson's Sapsucker
White-headed Woodpecker
Olive-sided Flycatcher
Willow Flycatcher (c)
Loggerhead Shrike
Pinyon Jay
Rufous Fantail (*mariae* ssp.) (d)
`Elepaio (d)
Tinian Monarch (d)
Horned Lark (*strigata* ssp.) (a)
`Oma`o
Golden White-eye (d)
Sage Thrasher
Virginia's Warbler
Green-tailed Towhee
Brewer's Sparrow
Oregon Vesper Sparrow (*affinis* ssp.)
Sage Sparrow
Black Rosy-Finch
Cassin's Finch
Hawai`i `Amakihi (d)
Oahu `Amakihi (d)
Kaua`i` `Amakihi (d)
`Anianiau (d)
`Akikiki (a,d)
Maui `Alauahio (d)
`Akeke`e (d)
`I`iwi (d)
`Apapane (d)

41 (a) ESA candidate, (b) ESA delisted, (c) non-listed subspecies or population of Threatened or Endangered species, (d) MBTA protection uncertain or lacking, (nb) non-breeding in this BCR

Table 40 USFWS Region 2 (Southwest Region) *BCC 2008* list.[42]

Lesser Prairie-Chicken (a)
Reddish Egret
Swallow-tailed Kite
Bald Eagle (b)
Common Black-Hawk
White-tailed Hawk
Golden Eagle
Peregrine Falcon (b)
Yellow Rail (nb)
Black Rail
Snowy Plover (c)
Wilson's Plover
Mountain Plover
American Oystercatcher
Solitary Sandpiper (nb)
Lesser Yellowlegs (nb)
Upland Sandpiper
Whimbrel (nb)
Long-billed Curlew
Hudsonian Godwit (nb)
Red Knot (*roselaari* ssp.) (nb)
Red Knot (*rufa* ssp.) (a) (nb)
Buff-breasted Sandpiper (nb)
Short-billed Dowitcher (nb)
Gull-billed Tern
Sandwich Tern
Black Skimmer
Yellow-billed Cuckoo (w. U.S. DPS) (a)
Flammulated Owl
Elf Owl
Burrowing Owl
Lucifer Hummingbird
Costa's Hummingbird
Lewis's Woodpecker
Red-headed Woodpecker
Gilded Flicker
Northern Beardless-Tyrannulet
Buff-breasted Flycatcher
Loggerhead Shrike
Bell's Vireo (c)

Gray Vireo
Pinyon Jay
Brown-headed Nuthatch
Sedge Wren (nb)
Wood Thrush
Bendire's Thrasher
LeConte's Thrasher
Sprague's Pipit (nb)
Olive Warbler
Colima Warbler
Lucy's Warbler
Yellow Warbler (*sonorana* ssp.)
Grace's Warbler
Prairie Warbler
Cerulean Warbler
Prothonotary Warbler
Worm-eating Warbler
Swainson's Warbler
Kentucky Warbler
Red-faced Warbler
Rufous-winged Sparrow
Bachman's Sparrow
Botteri's Sparrow
Five-striped Sparrow
Black-chinned Sparrow
Lark Bunting
Grasshopper Sparrow (*ammolegus* ssp.)
Baird's Sparrow (nb)
Henslow's Sparrow (nb)
LeConte's Sparrow (nb)
Nelson's Sharp-tailed Sparrow (nb)
Seaside Sparrow (c)
Harris's Sparrow (nb)
McCown's Longspur (nb)
Smith's Longspur (nb)
Chestnut-collared Longspur (nb)
Varied Bunting
Painted Bunting
Rusty Blackbird (nb)
Audubon's Oriole

42 (a) ESA candidate, (b) ESA delisted, (c) non-listed subspecies or population of Threatened or Endangered species, (d) MBTA protection uncertain or lacking, (nb) non-breeding in this BCR

Table 41 USFWS Region 3 (Great Lakes-Big Rivers Region) *BCC 2008* list.[43]

Pied-billed Grebe
Horned Grebe (nb)
American Bittern
Least Bittern
Bald Eagle (b)
Swainson's Hawk
Peregrine Falcon (b)
Yellow Rail
Black Rail
Solitary Sandpiper (nb)
Upland Sandpiper
Whimbrel (nb)
Hudsonian Godwit (nb)
Marbled Godwit
Red Knot (*roselaari* ssp.) (nb)
Red Knot (*rufa* ssp.) (a) (nb)
Buff-breasted Sandpiper (nb)
Short-billed Dowitcher (nb)
Black Tern
Common Tern
Black-billed Cuckoo
Short-eared Owl (nb)

Whip-poor-will
Red-headed Woodpecker
Olive-sided Flycatcher
Loggerhead Shrike
Bell's Vireo (c)
Bewick's Wren (*bewickii* ssp.)
Wood Thrush
Blue-winged Warbler
Golden-winged Warbler
Prairie Warbler
Cerulean Warbler
Worm-eating Warbler
Swainson's Warbler
Kentucky Warbler
Canada Warbler
Bachman's Sparrow
Henslow's Sparrow
Nelson's Sharp-tailed Sparrow
Smith's Longspur (nb)
Chestnut-collared Longspur
Dickcissel
Rusty Blackbird

---

43 (a) ESA candidate, (b) ESA delisted, (c) non-listed subspecies or population of Threatened or Endangered species, (d) MBTA protection uncertain or lacking, (nb) non-breeding in this BCR

Table 42 USFWS Region 4 (Southeast Region) mainland *BCC 2008* list.[44]

Red-throated Loon
Black-capped Petrel
Audubon's Shearwater
Band-rumped Storm-Petrel (a) (Hawaii DPS
is candidate; Atlantic pop. is not)
American Bittern
Least Bittern
Reddish Egret
Swallow-tailed Kite
Bald Eagle (b)
Short-tailed Hawk
American Kestrel (*paulus* ssp.)
Peregrine Falcon (b)
Yellow Rail
Black Rail
Limpkin
Snowy Plover (c)
Wilson's Plover
American Oystercatcher
Solitary Sandpiper (nb)
Whimbrel (nb)
Long-billed Curlew (nb)
Hudsonian Godwit (nb)
Marbled Godwit (nb)
Red Knot (*rufa* ssp.) (nb)
Semipalmated Sandpiper (Eastern) (nb)
Buff-breasted Sandpiper (nb)
Short-billed Dowitcher (nb)
Least Tern (c)
Gull-billed Tern
Black Skimmer
White-crowned Pigeon

Mangrove Cuckoo
Smooth-billed Ani
Short-eared Owl
Chuck-will's-widow
Red-headed Woodpecker
Olive-sided Flycatcher
Loggerhead Shrike
Black-whiskered Vireo
Brown-headed Nuthatch
Bewick's Wren (*bewickii* ssp.)
Sedge Wren
Wood Thrush
Sprague's Pipit
Blue-winged Warbler
Golden-winged Warbler
Prairie Warbler
Cerulean Warbler
Prothonotary Warbler
Worm-eating Warbler
Swainson's Warbler
Kentucky Warbler
Canada Warbler
Bachman's Sparrow
Henslow's Sparrow
LeConte's Sparrow
Nelson's Sharp-tailed Sparrow
Saltmarsh Sharp-tailed Sparrow
Seaside Sparrow (c)
Smith's Longspur
Painted Bunting
Rusty Blackbird

---

44 (a) ESA candidate, (b) ESA delisted, (c) non-listed subspecies or population of Threatened or Endangered species, (d) MBTA protection uncertain or lacking, (nb) non-breeding in this BCR

Table 43 USFWS Region 4 (Puerto Rico and U.S. Virgin Islands) *BCC 2008* list.[45]

West Indian Whistling-Duck
White-cheeked Pintail
Masked Duck
Ruddy Duck (*jamaicensis* ssp. only)
Audubon's Shearwater
Masked Booby
Brown Booby
Red-footed Booby
Magnificent Frigatebird
Least Bittern
American Flamingo
Black Rail
Yellow-breasted Crake
Caribbean Coot
Limpkin
Snowy Plover (c)
Wilson's Plover
American Oystercatcher
Red Knot (*rufa* ssp.) (a) (nb)
Semipalmated Sandpiper (Eastern) (nb)
White-crowned Pigeon
Bridled Quail-Dove
Antillean Mango (d)
Loggerhead Kingbird
Puerto Rican Vireo
Elfin-woods Warbler (a)
Greater Antillean Oriole

45 (a) ESA candidate, (b) ESA delisted, (c) non-listed subspecies or population of Threatened or Endangered species, (d) MBTA protection uncertain or lacking, (nb) non-breeding in this BCR

Table 44 USFWS Region 5 (Northeast Region) *BCC 2008* list.[46]

Red-throated Loon (nb)
Pied-billed Grebe
Horned Grebe (nb)
Greater Shearwater (nb)
Audubon's Shearwater (nb)
American Bittern
Least Bittern
Snowy Egret
Bald Eagle (b)
Peregrine Falcon (b)
Yellow Rail
Black Rail
Wilson's Plover
American Oystercatcher
Solitary Sandpiper (nb)
Lesser Yellowlegs (nb)
Upland Sandpiper
Whimbrel (nb)
Hudsonian Godwit (nb)
Marbled Godwit (nb)
Red Knot (*rufa* ssp.) (a) (nb)
Semipalmated Sandpiper (Eastern) (nb)
Purple Sandpiper (nb)
Buff-breasted Sandpiper (nb)
Short-billed Dowitcher (nb)
Least Tern (c)

Gull-billed Tern
Arctic Tern
Black Skimmer
Short-eared Owl (nb)
Whip-poor-will
Red-headed Woodpecker
Olive-sided Flycatcher
Loggerhead Shrike
Bewick's Wren (*bewickii* ssp.)
Sedge Wren
Bicknell's Thrush
Wood Thrush
Blue-winged Warbler
Golden-winged Warbler
Prairie Warbler
Bay-breasted Warbler
Cerulean Warbler
Worm-eating Warbler
Swainson's Warbler
Kentucky Warbler
Canada Warbler
Henslow's Sparrow
Nelson's Sharp-tailed Sparrow
Saltmarsh Sharp-tailed Sparrow
Seaside Sparrow (c)
Rusty Blackbird

---

46 (a) ESA candidate, (b) ESA delisted, (c) non-listed subspecies or population of Threatened or Endangered species, (d) MBTA protection uncertain or lacking, (nb) non-breeding in this BCR

Table 45 USFWS Region 6 (Mountain-Prairie Region) *BCC 2008* list.[47]

Gunnison Sage-Grouse
Lesser Prairie-Chicken (a)
Horned Grebe
American Bittern
Least Bittern
Bald Eagle (b)
Ferruginous Hawk
Golden Eagle
Peregrine Falcon (b)
Prairie Falcon
Yellow Rail
Black Rail
Snowy Plover (c)
Mountain Plover
Upland Sandpiper
Long-billed Curlew
Hudsonian Godwit (nb)
Marbled Godwit
Buff-breasted Sandpiper (nb)
Short-billed Dowitcher (nb)
Black-billed Cuckoo
Flammulated Owl
Burrowing Owl

Short-eared Owl
Lewis's Woodpecker
Red-headed Woodpecker
Willow Flycatcher (c)
Loggerhead Shrike
Bell's Vireo (c)
Gray Vireo
Pinyon Jay
Bewick's Wren (*bewickii* ssp.)
Sage Thrasher
Sprague's Pipit
Sage Sparrow
Grasshopper Sparrow
Baird's Sparrow
Henslow's Sparrow
Nelson's Sharp-tailed Sparrow
McCown's Longspur
Smith's Longspur
Chestnut-collared Longspur
Black Rosy-Finch
Brown-capped Rosy-Finch
Cassin's Finch

47 (a) ESA candidate, (b) ESA delisted, (c) non-listed subspecies or population of Threatened or Endangered species, (d) MBTA protection uncertain or lacking, (nb) non-breeding in this BCR

Table 46 USFWS Region 7 (Alaska Region) *BCC 2008* list.[48]

Red-throated Loon
Yellow-billed Loon
Horned Grebe
Laysan Albatross
Black-footed Albatross
Red-faced Cormorant
Pelagic Cormorant
Northern Goshawk (*laingi* ssp.)
Peregrine Falcon (b)
Black Oystercatcher
Solitary Sandpiper
Lesser Yellowlegs
Whimbrel
Bristle-thighed Curlew
Hudsonian Godwit
Bar-tailed Godwit
Marbled Godwit
Red Knot (*roselaari* ssp.)
Rock Sandpiper (*ptilocnemis* spp.)
Dunlin (*arcticola* ssp.)
Buff-breasted Sandpiper
Short-billed Dowitcher
Red-legged Kittiwake
Aleutian Tern
Arctic Tern
Marbled Murrelet (c)
Kittlitz's Murrelet (a)
Whiskered Auklet
Rufous Hummingbird
Olive-sided Flycatcher
Smith's Longspur
McKay's Bunting
Rusty Blackbird

---

48 (a) ESA candidate, (b) ESA delisted, (c) non-listed subspecies or population of Threatened or Endangered species, (d) MBTA protection uncertain or lacking, (nb) non-breeding in this BCR

Table 47 USFWS Region 8 (California and Nevada) *BCC 2008* list.[49]

Black-footed Albatross
Pink-footed Shearwater (nb)
Ashy Storm-Petrel
Bald Eagle (b)
Peregrine Falcon (b)
Yellow Rail
Black Rail
Snowy Plover (c)
Mountain Plover (nb)
Black Oystercatcher
Whimbrel (nb)
Long-billed Curlew (nb)
Marbled Godwit (nb)
Red Knot (*roselaari* ssp.) (nb)
Short-billed Dowitcher (nb)
Gull-billed Tern
Black Skimmer
Xantus's Murrelet (a)
Yellow-billed Cuckoo (w. US DPS) (a)
Flammulated Owl
Burrowing Owl
Spotted Owl (*occidentalis* ssp.) (c)
Black Swift
Costa's Hummingbird
Calliope Hummingbird
Allen's Hummingbird
Lewis's Woodpecker
Williamson's Sapsucker

Olive-sided Flycatcher
Willow Flycatcher (c)
Loggerhead Shrike
Bell's Vireo (c)
Gray Vireo
Island Scrub-Jay
Pinyon Jay
Yellow-billed Magpie
Oak Titmouse
Cactus Wren
Sage Thrasher
LeConte's Thrasher
Virginia's Warbler
Yellow Warbler (*brewsteri* ssp.)
Yellow Warbler (*sonorana* ssp.)
Common Yellowthroat (*sinuosa* ssp.)
Green-tailed Towhee
Spotted Towhee (*clementae* ssp.)
Brewer's Sparrow
Black-chinned Sparrow
Sage Sparrow
Song Sparrow (*graminea* ssp.)
Song Sparrow (*maxillaris* ssp.)
Song Sparrow (*pusillula* ssp.)
Song Sparrow (*samuelis* ssp.)
Tricolored Blackbird
Lawrence's Goldfinch

---

49 (a) ESA candidate, (b) ESA delisted, (c) non-listed subspecies or population of Threatened or Endangered species, (d) MBTA protection uncertain or lacking, (nb) non-breeding in this BCR

Table 48 National (including Caribbean and Pacific Island "Territories") *BCC 2008* list.[50]

West Indian Whistling-Duck
Greater Sage-Grouse (Colum. Basin DPS) (a)
Gunnison Sage-Grouse
Lesser Prairie-Chicken (a)
Yellow-billed Loon
Black-footed Albatross
Tahiti Petrel (d)
Phoenix Petrel (d)
Black-capped Petrel
Pink-footed Shearwater
Christmas Shearwater
Audubon's Shearwater
Polynesian Storm-Petrel (d)
Ashy Storm-Petrel
Band-rumped Storm-Petrel (a) (Hawaii DPS is
    candidate; Atlantic pop. is not)
Reddish Egret
Swallow-tailed Kite
Bald Eagle (b)
Swainson's Hawk
Peregrine Falcon (b)
Yellow Rail
Black Rail
Spotless Crake (Am. Samoa pop.) (a, d)
Caribbean Coot
Limpkin
Snowy Plover (c)
Wilson's Plover
Mountain Plover
American Oystercatcher
Black Oystercatcher
Solitary Sandpiper
Lesser Yellowlegs
Upland Sandpiper
Whimbrel
Bristle-thighed Curlew
Long-billed Curlew
Hudsonian Godwit

Bar-tailed Godwit
Marbled Godwit
Red Knot (*roselaari* ssp.)
Red Knot (*rufa* ssp.) (a) (nb)
Semipalmated Sandpiper (Eastern) (nb)
Purple Sandpiper (nb)
Rock Sandpiper (*ptilocnemis* ssp.)
Dunlin (*arcticola* spp.)
Buff-breasted Sandpiper
Short-billed Dowitcher
Red-legged Kittiwake
Aleutian Tern
Least Tern (c)
Gull-billed Tern
Black Skimmer
Marbled Murrelet (c)
Kittlitz's Murrelet (a)
Xantus's Murrelet (a)
White-crowned Pigeon
Friendly Ground-Dove (Am. Samoa) (a,d)
Green Parakeet (d)
Red-crowned Parrot (d)
Yellow-billed Cuckoo (w. U.S. DPS) (a)
Mangrove Cuckoo
Flammulated Owl
Elf Owl
Spotted Owl (*occidentalis* ssp.) (c)
Short-eared Owl
Black Swift
Costa's Hummingbird
Calliope Hummingbird
Rufous Hummingbird
Allen's Hummingbird
Elegant Trogon
Lewis's Woodpecker
Red-headed Woodpecker
Table 48 Continued

50 (a) ESA candidate, (b) ESA delisted, (c) non-listed subspecies or population of Threatened or Endangered species, (d) MBTA protection uncertain or lacking, (nb) non-breeding in this BCR

Nuttall's Woodpecker
Arizona Woodpecker
White-headed Woodpecker
Olive-sided Flycatcher
Willow Flycatcher (c)
Loggerhead Shrike
Puerto Rican Vireo
Bell's Vireo (c)
Gray Vireo
Island Scrub-Jay
Pinyon Jay
Yellow-billed Magpie
Rufous Fantail (*mariae* ssp.) (d)
`Elepaio (d)
Tinian Monarch (d)
Horned Lark (*strigata* ssp.) (a)
Oak Titmouse
Brown-headed Nuthatch
Bewick's Wren (*bewickii* ssp.)
`Omao
Bicknell's Thrush
Wood Thrush
Golden White-eye (d)
Bendire's Thrasher
LeConte's Thrasher
Sprague's Pipit
Blue-winged Warbler
Golden-winged Warbler
Virginia's Warbler
Colima Warbler
Lucy's Warbler
Grace's Warbler
Prairie Warbler
Bay-breasted Warbler
Cerulean Warbler
Elfin-woods Warbler (a)
Prothonotary Warbler
Worm-eating Warbler
Swainson's Warbler
Kentucky Warbler
Canada Warbler
Red-faced Warbler

Bachman's Sparrow
Five-striped Sparrow
Brewer's Sparrow
Black-chinned Sparrow
Baird's Sparrow
Henslow's Sparrow
Nelson's Sharp-tailed Sparrow
Saltmarsh Sharp-tailed Sparrow
Seaside Sparrow (c)
Harris's Sparrow
McCown's Longspur
Smith's Longspur
McKay's Bunting
Varied Bunting
Painted Bunting
Dickcissel
Tricolored Blackbird
Rusty Blackbird
Audubon's Oriole
Black Rosy-Finch
Brown-capped Rosy-Finch
Lawrence's Goldfinch
Hawai`i `Amakihi (d)
Oahu `Amakihi (d)
Kaua`i `Amakihi (d)
`Anianiau (d)
`Akikiki (a,d)
Maui `Alauahio (d)
`Akek`ee (d)
`I`iwi (d)
`Apapane (d)

Rufous-winged Sparrow

Appendix B

Matrix of Species on BCR, USFWS Region, and National Lists in *BCC 2008*,
Arranged Taxonomically (according to American Ornithologists' Union 48th Checklist)[51]

---

51 (a) ESA candidate, (b) ESA delisted, (c) non-listed subspecies or population of threatened or endangered species, (d) <u>MBTA protection uncertain or lacking</u>

Bird Conservation Regions

'x' indicates species is included for breeding period (plus non-breeding where species occurs year-round), 'nb' indicates species is included only for non-breeding period

Species	1	2	3	4	5	9	10	11	12	13	14	15	16	17	18	19	20	21	22	23	24	25	26	27	28	29	30	31	32	33	34	35	36	37	U.S. Pacif. Islds.	U.S. Carib. Islds.	USFWS R1	R2	R3	R4	R4a	R5	R6	R7	R8	National
West Indian Whistling-Duck																																				x				+						+
White-cheeked Pintail																																				x		+		+	+					
Masked Duck																																				x		+		+	+					
Ruddy Duck (*jamaicensis* ssp. only)																																				x		+		+	+					+
Greater Sage-Grouse (Columbia Basin DPS)(a)						x																															+									+
Gunnison Sage-Grouse													x																														+			+
Lesser Prairie-Chicken (a)															x	x																						+					+			+
Red-throated Loon				nb							nb													nb			nb																			
Yellow-billed Loon				nb																																								+		+
Pied-billed Grebe								x	nb	nb	nb								x	x																						+				
Horned Grebe							x	nb	nb				x														nb												+			+	+			
Eared Grebe						nb																																								
Western Grebe					nb	nb																																								
Laysan Albatross	nb	nb		nb	nb																														x								+	+		
Black-footed Albatross				nb	nb																						nb								x		+						+	+		+
Herald Petrel																																			x		+									
Tahiti Petrel (d)																																			x		+									+
Phoenix Petrel (d)																																			x		+									+
Black-capped Petrel																											nb													+						+
Pink-footed Shearwater					nb																						nb										+								+	+
Greater Shearwater											nb																nb															+				
Christmas Shearwater																																	x		x		+									+
Black-vented Shearwater					nb																						nb																			
Audubon's Shearwater																								nb			nb	nb							x	x				+		+				+
Polynesian Storm-Petrel (d)																											x								x		+									+
Ashy Storm-Petrel																											x																		+	+

(4a = Puerto Rico & USVI)

Bird Conservation Regions

'x' indicates species is included for breeding period (plus non-breeding where species occurs year-round), 'nb' indicates species is included only for non-breeding period

(4a = Puerto Rico & USVI)

Species	BCR 1	2	3	4	5	9	10	11	12	13	14	15	16	17	18	19	20	21	22	23	24	25	26	27	28	29	30	31	32	33	34	35	36	37	U.S. Pacif. Islds.	U.S. Carib. Islds.	USFWS R1	R2	R3	R4	R4a	R5	R6	R7	R8	National
Band-rumped Storm-Petrel (a) (Hawaii DPS is candidate; Atlantic pop. is not)																																	nb	x			+									+
Tristram's Storm-Petrel																																		x				+								
Masked Booby																									nb											x					+					
Brown Booby																																				x				+						+
Red-footed Booby																																				x				+						+
Great Cormorant									nb																																					
Red-faced Cormorant	x	x			x																																							+		
Pelagic Cormorant (*pelagicus* ssp.)	x	x			x																																							+		
Magnificent Frigatebird																											x						nb	x		x				+						
American Bittern							x	x	x	x		x	x	x						x	x		x	x		x	x		x	x	nb	nb				+	+	+		+	+	+			
Least Bittern							x	x	x	x	x	x								x	x		x	x		x	x		x	x		x				+	+	+	+	+					
Snowy Egret											x									x							x													+					
Little Blue Heron																x			x																	+										
Reddish Egret																									x		x					x				x		+								+
Black-crowned Night-Heron									x											x																										
Roseate Spoonbill																									nb		x																			
American Flamingo																																				x				+						+
Swallow-tailed Kite																				x			x		x		x													+						+
Mississippi Kite																	x		x																					+						
Bald Eagle (b)	x	x	x	x	x	x	x	x	x	x	x	x	x	x	x	x	x	nb	x	x	x	x	x	x	x	x	x	x	x	x	x	x	x	x			+	+	+	+	+	+	+	+	+	+
Northern Goshawk (*laingi* ssp.)					x																																							+		
Common Black-Hawk																														x	x							+								
Harris's Hawk																																x														
Short-tailed Hawk																												x				x								+						
Swainson's Hawk					x	x																										x	x					+								+

'x' indicates species is included for breeding period (plus non-breeding where species occurs year-round), **'nb'** indicates species is included only for non-breeding period

(4a = Puerto Rico & USVI)

Species	BCR 1	2	3	4	5	9	10	11	12	13	14	15	16	17	18	19	20	21	22	23	24	25	26	27	28	29	30	31	32	33	34	35	36	37	U.S. Pacif. Islds.	U.S. Carib. Islds.	USFWS 1	2	3	4	4a	5	6	7	8	National
White-tailed Hawk																																	x					+								
Ferruginous Hawk						x	x						x	x		x															nb							+								+
Golden Eagle						x							x	x	x																	x						+								+
American Kestrel (*paulus* ssp.)																	x			x																				+						+
Peregrine Falcon (b)	x	x	x	x	x	x	x	x	x		x	x	x	x	x		x	x	x	x	x	x	x	x				x			nb		nb				+	+	+	+	+	+	+	+	+	+
Prairie Falcon													x		x																									+						
Yellow Rail						x					x		x	x			x			nb	nb	nb		nb				nb					nb					+	+	+	+	+				+
Black Rail															x			nb	x	x	x	x	x	x	x	x	x	x					x			x	+	+	+	+	+	+	+			+
Spotless Crake (American Samoa pop.) (a,d)																																			x							+				+
Yellow-breasted Crake																																				x						+				+
Purple Swamphen																																			x											+
Caribbean Coot																																				x						+				+
Limpkin																			x					x				x								x					+	+				+
Snowy Plover (c)						x		x	x		x	x			x		x		x	x	x	x	x	x	x	x		x	x	x			x			x	+	+	+	+	+	+		+		+
Wilson's Plover																				x	x	x	x	x			x	x	x				x			x			+	+	+	+				+
Mountain Plover													nb	nb	x	nb	x											nb					nb				+	+					+			+
American Oystercatcher											x									x	x	x	x	x			x	x					x			x	+		+	+	+	+				+
Black Oystercatcher	x	x			x																											x					+							+		+
Solitary Sandpiper		x	x	nb	nb	nb		nb	nb	nb	nb									nb				nb				nb			nb	nb	nb	nb											+	+
Lesser Yellowlegs		x	x	nb	nb	nb		nb	nb	nb	nb									nb				nb				nb			nb	nb	nb	nb										+	+	+
Upland Sandpiper				x		x				x				x	x		nb			nb	nb							nb			nb	nb	nb						+				+	+	+	+
Whimbrel																				nb				nb				nb					nb		nb									+		+
Bristle-thighed Curlew	x		x	x	x	x		x																										nb	nb									+		+

Bird Conservation Regions

'X' indicates species is included for breeding period (plus non-breeding where species occurs year-round), 'nb' indicates species is included only for non-breeding period

(4a = Puerto Rico & USVI)

Species	1	2	3	4	5	9	10	11	12	13	14	15	16	17	18	19	20	21	22	23	24	25	26	27	28	29	30	31	32	33	34	35	36	37	U.S. Pacif. Islds.	U.S. Carib. Islds.	R1	R2	R3	R4	R4a	R5	R6	R7	R8	National
Long-billed Curlew													x	x	x	x	x																									+				+
Hudsonian Godwit	x			x	nb		nb	nb	nb		nb				nb	nb				nb							nb				x						+	+	+	+	+	+			+	+
Bar-tailed Godwit	x	x			nb		nb	nb	nb																																			+	+
Marbled Godwit	x				nb	nb	x	nb	nb				x		nb	nb				nb			nb				nb				x						+	+	+	+	+	+	+	+	+	+
Red Knot (*roselaari* ssp.)	x	x	x	x	nb	nb	x	nb	nb						nb	nb				nb			nb				nb				x						+							+	+	+
Red Knot (*rufa* ssp.) (a)								nb	nb	nb					nb	nb				nb	nb		nb				nb				nb					nb	+	+	+	+	+	+	+	+	+	+
Semipalmated Sandpiper (Eastern)								nb	nb	nb					nb					nb	nb		nb				nb				nb					nb				+	+	+		+		+
Purple Sandpiper								nb												nb																				+	+				+
Rock Sandpiper (*ptilocnemis*)	x	nb	nb																																									+	+
Dunlin (*arcticola*)	nb	x																																										+	+
Buff-breasted Sandpiper		x			nb	nb	nb	nb	nb		nb				nb	nb				nb	nb	nb	nb				nb				nb						+	+	+	+	+	+	+	+	+	+
Short-billed Dowitcher	x			x	nb	nb	nb	nb	nb		nb				nb	nb				nb	nb		nb				nb				nb						+	+	+	+	+	+	+	+	+	+
Red-legged Kittiwake	x																																												+
Aleutian Tern	x	x		x																x							x				x													+	+
Least Tern (c)									nb																		x			x	x										+			+	+
Gull-billed Tern					nb															x	x		x				x													+	+	+				+
Caspian Tern			x																																					+	+					
Black Tern		x						x	x											x	x																								
Common Tern		x						x	x											x	x																								
Arctic Tern	x	x	x		x				x																																				
Sandwich Tern									nb														x				x														+				
Black Skimmer																				x	x		x				x				x										+				+
Marbled Murrelet (c)	x	x		x	x															x	x		x				x				x										+				+

72

Bird Conservation Regions

(4a = Puerto Rico & USVI)

Species	1	2	3	4	5	9	10	11	12	13	14	15	16	17	18	19	20	21	22	23	24	25	26	27	28	29	30	31	32	33	34	35	36	37	U.S. Pacif. Islds.	U.S. Carib. Islds.	R1	R2	R3	R4	R4a	R5	R6	R7	R8	National
Kittlitz's Murrelet (a)	x	x																																											+		+
Xantus's Murrelet (a)					x																																								+	+
Cassin's Auklet																																														
Whiskered Auklet	x																																											+		
White-crowned Pigeon																												x								x				+						+
Red-billed Pigeon																																x						+							
Common Ground-Dove																								x				x												+						
Bridled Quail-Dove																																				x					+					+
Friendly Ground-Dove (American Samoa DPS) (a,d)																																			x		+									
Green Parakeet (d)																																	x					+							+
Red-crowned Parrot (d)																																	x					+							+
Yellow-billed Cuckoo (w. U.S. DPS) (a)						x	x	x				x	x																x	x	x						+	+					+		+	+
Mangrove Cuckoo																												x												+						+
Black-billed Cuckoo								x		x	x		x	x						x	x																		+				+			
Smooth-billed Ani																					x							x												+						
Flammulated Owl						x	x					x	x																x	x	x												+		+	
Elf Owl																														x	x	x	x					+							
Burrowing Owl						x	x	x					x	x	x														x	x	x								+				+		+	
Spotted Owl (occidentalis ssp.) (c)					x							x																	x								+								+	+
Short-eared Owl							nb	nb	nb			x	x		nb	nb		nb nb				nb				nb	nb							nb x									+			+
Northern Saw-whet Owl (S. Appalachian breeding pop.)																						x		x																						
Chuck-will's-widow												x							x									x													+					
Whip-poor-will													x		x					x x x x							x													+				
Black Swift	x x x					x x x						x x																	x																+

73

Bird Conservation Regions

'x' indicates species is included for breeding period (plus non-breeding where species occurs year-round), 'nb' indicates species is included only for non-breeding period

Species	BCRs (where 'x' appears)	U.S. Pacif. Islds.	U.S. Carib. Islds.	USFWS Regions (where '+' appears)	National
Antillean Mango (d)			x	4a	
Buff-bellied Hummingbird				2	
Blue-throated Hummingbird	34, 36				
Lucifer Hummingbird	35			2	
Costa's Hummingbird	32, 33			1, 2	+
Calliope Hummingbird	5, 9, 10, 15			1, 2, 6	+
Rufous Hummingbird	5			7	+
Allen's Hummingbird	5, 32			1	+
Elegant Trogon	34			2	+
Lewis's Woodpecker	5, 9, 10, 11, 12, 14, 16, 17, 32, 33			1, 2, 6	+
Red-headed Woodpecker	11, 12, 13, 17, 18, 19, 22, 23, 24, 25, 26, 27, 28, 29, 30, 31			3, 4, 5, 6	+
Gila Woodpecker	33				
Williamson's Sapsucker	5, 9, 15, 16, 33			1	+
Yellow-bellied Sapsucker (S. Appalachian breeding pop.)	28				
Nuttall's Woodpecker	32				
Arizona Woodpecker	34			2	+
White-headed Woodpecker	5, 9, 10, 33			1	+
Northern Flicker	22				
Gilded Flicker	33			2	
Northern Beardless-Tyrannulet	36			2	
Olive-sided Flycatcher	9, 10, 14, 28, 34			1, 2, 3	+
Acadian Flycatcher	14, 22, 27				
Willow Flycatcher (c)	5, 9, 10, 14, 16, 21			1, 2, 6	+
Buff-breasted Flycatcher				2	
Loggerhead Kingbird			x		
Scissor-tailed Flycatcher	19, 20, 21				

(4a = Puerto Rico & USVI)

74

Bird Conservation Regions

'X' indicates species is included for breeding period (plus non-breeding where species occurs year-round), 'nb' indicates species is included only for non-breeding period

Species	1	2	3	4	5	9	10	11	12	13	14	15	16	17	18	19	20	21	22	23	24	25	26	27	28	29	30	31	32	33	34	35	36	37	U.S. Pacif. Islds.	U.S. Carib. Islds.	R1	R2	R3	R4	R4a	R5	R6	R7	R8	National
Rose-throated Becard																																														
Micronesian Myzomela (d)																														x					X		+							+		+
Loggerhead Shrike						x	x						x		x	x	x	x	x	x	x									x	x						+	+	+				+	+	+	+
Puerto Rican Vireo																																				X				+					+
Bell's Vireo (c)													x		x	x	x	x	x		x								x	x	x						+	+	+				+		+
Gray Vireo													x				x													x								+					+		+
Black-whiskered Vireo																												x												+					
Island Scrub-Jay																													x								+								+
Pinyon Jay						x							x	x																x	x						+	+					+		+
Yellow-billed Magpie																													x								+							+	+
Rufous Fantail (*mariae* ssp.) (d)																																			X		+									+
Rufous Fantail (*saipanensis* ssp.) (d)																																			X		+									
Elepaio (d)																																			X		+									+
Fiji Shrikebill (d)																																			X											
Tinian Monarch (d)																																			X		+									+
Horned Lark (*strigata* ssp.) (a)					x																																+									+
Black-capped Chickadee (S. Appalachian pop.)																																														
Oak Titmouse																													x								+								+
Juniper Titmouse														x																																
Verdin																														x																
Brown-headed Nuthatch																								x				x												+					+
Cactus Wren																													x								+								+
Bewick's Wren (*bewickii* ssp.)																			x	x	x	x		x	x	x	x										+	+	+	+		+	+		
Sedge Wren																			nb	nb	nb	x		nb	nb	nb	x						nb				+		+			+			
Marsh Wren																			x																											

Legend column groups (right of Bird Conservation Regions): USFWS Regions (4a = Puerto Rico & USVI), National.

Bird Conservation Regions

'x' indicates species is included for breeding period (plus non-breeding where species occurs year-round), 'nb' indicates species is included only for non-breeding period

(4a = Puerto Rico & USVI)

Species	1	2	3	4	5	6	7	8	9	10	11	12	13	14	15	16	17	18	19	20	21	22	23	24	25	26	27	28	29	30	31	32	33	34	35	36	37	67	U.S. Pacif. Islds.	U.S. Carib. Islds.	R1	R2	R3	R4	4a	R5	R6	R7	R8	National
'Omao																																						x												+
Veery																x																														+				+
Bicknell's Thrush														x																																				
Wood Thrush												x	x	x								x	x	x	x	x	x	x	x	x												+	+	+		+				+
Bridled White-eye (saypani ssp. only) (c,d)																																							x											
Golden White-eye (d)																																							x		+									+
Sage Thrasher									x	x																																					+			
Brown Thrasher																						x																												
Bendire's Thrasher																																x	x	x								+								+
Curve-billed Thrasher																																		x																
LeConte's Thrasher																																x	x									+								+
Micronesian Starling (guami ssp.) (d)																																							x											
Polynesian Starling (d)																																							x											
Sprague's Pipit											x						x	nb		nb		nb													nb	nb	nb					+								+
Phainopepla																																	x	x																
Olive Warbler																																		x								+								
Blue-winged Warbler													x	x								x	x	x			x	x	x	x													+	+		+				+
Golden-winged Warbler												x	x										x	x				x															+	+		+				+
Virginia's Warbler									x																								x	x								+					+			+
Colima Warbler																																		x								+								+
Lucy's Warbler																																	x	x								+							+	+
Tropical Parula																				x																x														
Yellow Warbler (brewsteri)																																x																		
Yellow Warbler (gundlachii ssp.)																																								x										
Yellow Warbler (sonorana)																																	x	x	x															

76

Bird Conservation Regions

'x' indicates species is included for breeding period (plus non-breeding where species occurs year-round), 'nb' indicates species is included only for non-breeding period

Species	1	2	3	4	5	9	10	11	12	13	14	15	16	17	18	19	20	21	22	23	24	25	26	27	28	29	30	31	32	33	34	35	36	37	U.S. Pacif. Islds.	U.S. Carib. Islds.	R1	R2	R3	R4	R4a	R5	R6	R7	R8	National
Black-throated Gray Warbler																														x																
Black-throated Green Warbler										x	x													x	x																					+
Grace's Warbler													x																		x	x						+								+
Prairie Warbler										x	x								x	x	x	x	x	x	x	x	x											+	+	+	+					+
Bay-breasted Warbler											x																												+		+				+
Cerulean Warbler										x									x	x	x	x	x	x	x	x	x											+	+	+	+					+
Elfin-woods Warbler (a)																																				x					x					+
Prothonotary Warbler																		x	x	x	x	x	x	x	x	x	x						x					+	+	+	+					+
Worm-eating Warbler																			x	x	x	x	x	x	x	x													+	+	+					+
Swainson's Warbler																		x	x	x	x	x	x	x	x	x												+	+	+	+					+
Louisiana Waterthrush																			x	x	x	x	x	x	x	x													+	+	+					
Kentucky Warbler																		x	x	x	x	x	x	x	x	x												+	+	+	+					+
Common Yellowthroat (*sinuosa* ssp.)																													x																	
Canada Warbler								x	x	x															x														+			+				+
Red-faced Warbler																									x						x							+								+
Summer Tanager																									x							x	x													
White-collared Seedeater																									x							x	x													
Green-tailed Towhee					x								x																																	
Spotted Towhee (*clementae* ssp.)																												x							+										+	
Canyon Towhee																										x	x																		
Rufous-winged Sparrow																									x	x											+								
Cassin's Sparrow							x																	x	x							x	x					+								+
Bachman's Sparrow										x												x	x	x	x		x											+	+						
Botteri's Sparrow																								x	x				x			x	x					+								+
Rufous-crowned Sparrow																x													x	x																

77

Bird Conservation Regions

'X' indicates species is included for breeding period (plus non-breeding where species occurs year-round), 'nb' indicates species is included only for non-breeding period

(4a = Puerto Rico & USVI)

Species	1	2	3	4	5	9	10	11	12	13	14	15	16	17	18	19	20	21	22	23	24	25	26	27	28	29	30	31	32	33	34	35	36	37	U.S. Pacif. Islds.	U.S. Carib. Islds.	R1	R2	R3	R4	R4a	R5	R6	R7	R8	National
Five-striped Sparrow																														x								+									+
Brewer's Sparrow						x	x					x	x																								+	+							+	+
Field Sparrow													x	x		x																							+							
Black-chinned Sparrow						x																							x	x	x							+								+
Oregon Vesper Sparrow (*affinis* ssp.)					x																																+									
Sage Sparrow						x	x					x	x																x	x							+	+								+
Lark Bunting							x	x						x	x																nb	nb	nb	nb									+			
Grasshopper Sparrow												x	x	x	x				x										x		nb												+			
Grasshopper Sparrow (*ammolegus* ssp.)																															nb							+								+
Baird's Sparrow								x					x	x																	nb	nb											+			+
Henslow's Sparrow									x	x							nb	x	x	x	nb	x	x	x	nb							nb	nb					+	+				+			+
LeConte's Sparrow																	nb		nb	x	x			x	nb							nb	nb						+							
Nelson's Sharp-tailed Sparrow											x						nb		nb					x	nb							nb	nb					+	+	+	+		+			+
Saltmarsh Sharp-tailed Sparrow											x						nb		nb					x	nb							nb	nb							+	+		+			+
Seaside Sparrow (c)																	x		x	x	x			x	x							nb								+	+		+			+
Song Sparrow (*graminea* ssp.)																													x																	
Song Sparrow (*maxillaris* ssp.)																													x																	
Song Sparrow (*pusillula* ssp.)																													x																	
Song Sparrow (*samuelis* ssp.)																													x								+									
Harris's Sparrow																	nb	nb	nb		nb		nb	nb							nb	nb						+					+			+
McCown's Longspur												x	x			x	x	nb	nb		nb	nb										nb						+					+			+
Smith's Longspur	x	x											nb			nb			nb	nb																			+					+	+	+
Chestnut-collared Longspur													nb		x	x	nb	x	x	nb	nb										nb	nb	nb											+		
McKay's Bunting	x	nb																																										+		+

Bird Conservation Regions

'x' indicates species is included for breeding period (plus non-breeding where species occurs year-round), 'nb' indicates species is included only for non-breeding period

(4a = Puerto Rico & USVI)

Species	1	2	3	4	5	9	10	11	12	13	14	15	16	17	18	19	20	21	22	23	24	25	26	27	28	29	30	31	32	33	34	35	36	37	U.S. Pacif. Islds.	U.S. Carib. Islds.	R1	R2	R3	R4	R4a	R5	R6	R7	R8	National
Varied Bunting																															x	x	x					+								+
Painted Bunting																												nb			x	x	x	x				+		+						+
Dickcissel								x					x						x	x	x										x	x							+							+
Bobolink								x												x																					a				+	
Tricolored Blackbird											x																		x								+									+
Rusty Blackbird									x		x								nb	nb	nb		nb	nb	nb		nb	nb											+		a	+				+
Greater Antillean Oriole																																				x					a					
Orchard Oriole																		x	x	x		x	x	x																						
Hooded Oriole													x																	x		x														
Altamira Oriole													x																			x														
Audubon's Oriole																														x		x						+								+
Black Rosy-Finch						x	x						x																														+			+
Brown-capped Rosy-Finch													x																														+			+
Purple Finch				x		x			x																																					
Cassin's Finch							x					x	x																														+			
Red Crossbill (S. Appalachian pop.)																									x																					
Lawrence's Goldfinch																													x	x							+									+
Hawai'i 'Amakihi (d)																																			x		+									+
Oahu 'Amakihi (d)																																			x		+									+
Kaua'i 'Amakihi (d)																																			x		+									+
Anianiau (d)																																			x		+									+
'Akikiki (a,d)																																			x		+									+
Maui 'Alauahio (d)																																			x		+									+
'Akeke'e (d)																																			x		+									+
'I'iwi (d)																																			x		+									+
'Apapane (d)																																			x		+									+

79

Bird Conservation Regions | **USFWS Regions** | **National**

'X' indicates species is included for breeding period (plus non-breeding where species occurs year-round), 'nb' indicates species is included only for non-breeding period

(4a = Puerto Rico & USVI)

BCR	1	2	3	4	5	9	10	11	12	13	14	15	16	17	18	19	20	21	22	23	24	25	26	27	28	29	30	31	32	33	34	35	36	37	U.S. Pacif. Islds.	U.S. Carib. Islds.	USFWS 1	2	3	4	4a	5	6	7	8	National
Totals	13	22	10	14	30	28	22	27	23	27	29	11	27	28	16	26	11	19	39	30	26	27	53	25	18	45	48	45	28	37	31	31	42	18	20	27	61	78	45	19	27	51	45	34	55	147

(a) ESA candidate, (b) ESA delisted, (c) non-listed subspecies or population of ESA listed species, (d) MBTA protection uncertain or lacking

APPENDIX C

Index of Scientific Names of Species Appearing in the BCC 2008 Lists
(Tables 2-48), Arranged Alphabetically by Common Name

Common Name	Scientific Name
Akekee	*Loxops caeruleirostris*
Akikiki	*Oreomystis bairdi*
Alauahio, Maui	*Paroreomyza maculata*
Albatross, Black-footed	*Phoebastria nigripes*
Albatross, Laysan	*Phoebastria immutabilis*
Amakihi, Hawaii	*Hemignathus virens*
Amakihi, Kauai	*Hemignathus kauaiensis*
Amakihi, Oahu	*Hemignathus flavus*
Ani, Smooth-billed	*Crotophaga ani*
Anianiau	*Hemignathus pan/us*
Apapane	*Mimatione sanguinea*
Auklet, Cassin's	*Ptychororamphus aleuticus*
Auklet, Whiskered	*Aethia pygmaea*
Beardless-Tyrannulet, Northern	*Camptostoma imberbe*
Becard, Rose-throated	*Pachyramphus aglaiae*
Bittern, American	*Botaurus lentiginosus*
Bittern, Least	*Ixobrychus exilis*
Blackbird, Rusty	*Euphagus carolinus*
Blackbird, Tricolored	*Agelaius tricolor*
Black-Hawk, Common	*Buteogallus anthracinus*
Bobolink	*Dolichonyx oryzivorus*
Booby, Brown	*Sula leucogaster*
Booby, Masked	*Sula dactylatra*
Booby, Red-footed	*Sula sula*
Bunting, Lark	*Calamospiza melanocorys*
Bunting, McKay's	*Plectrophenax hyperboreus*
Bunting, Painted	*Passerina ciris*
Bunting, Varied	*Passerina versicolor*
Chickadee, Black-capped	*Poecile atricapillus*
Chuck-will's-widow	*Caprimulgus carolinensis*
Coot, Caribbean	*Fulica caribaea*
Cormorant, Great	*Phalacrocorax carbo*
Cormorant, Red-faced	*Phalacrocorax urile*
Cormorant, Pelagic	*Phalacrocorax pelagicus pelagicus*
Crake, Spotless	*Porzana tabuensis*
Crake, Yellow-breasted	*Porzana flaviventer*
Crossbill, Red	*Loxia curvirostra*
Cuckoo, Black-billed	*Coccyzus erythropthalmus*
Cuckoo, Mangrove	*Coccyzus minor*
Cuckoo, Yellow-billed	*Coccyzus americanus*
Curlew, Bristle-thighed	*Numenius tahitiensis*
Curlew, Long-billed	*Numenius americanus*
Dickcissel	*Spiza americana*
Dowitcher, Short-billed	*Limnodromus griseus*
Duck, Masked	*Nomonyx dominicus*

Duck, Ruddy	*Oxyura jamaicensis jamaicensis*
Dunlin	*Calidris alpina arcticola*
Eagle, Bald	*Haliaeetus leucocephalus*
Eagle, Golden	*Aquila chrysaetos*
Egret, Reddish	*Egretta rufescens*
Egret, Snowy	*Egretta thula*
Elepaio	*Chasiempis sandwichensis*
Falcon, Peregrine	*Falco peregrinus*
Falcon, Prairie	*Falco mexicanus*
Fantail, Rufous	*Rhipidura rufifrons mariae*
Fantail, Rufous	*Rhipidura rufifrons saipanensis*
Finch, Cassin's	*Carpodacus cassinii*
Finch, Purple	*Carpodacus purpureus*
Flamingo, American	*Phoenicopterus ruber*
Flicker, Gilded	*Colaptes chrysoides*
Flicker, Northern	*Colaptes auratus*
Flycatcher, Acadian	*Empidonax virescens*
Flycatcher, Buff-breasted	*Empidonax fulvifrons*
Flycatcher, Olive-sided	*Contopus cooperi*
Flycatcher, Scissor-tailed	*Tyrannus forficatus*
Flycatcher, Willow	*Empidonax traillii*
Frigatebird, Magnificent	*Fregata magnificens*
Godwit, Bar-tailed	*Limosa lapponica baueri*
Godwit, Hudsonian	*Limosa haemastica*
Godwit, Marbled	*Limosa fedoa*
Goldfinch, Lawrence's	*Carduelis lawrencei*
Goshawk, Northern	*Accipiter gentilis laingi*
Grebe, Eared	*Podiceps nigricollis*
Grebe, Horned	*Podiceps auritus*
Grebe, Pied-billed	*Podilymbus podiceps*
Grebe, Western	*Aechmophorus occidentalis*
Ground-Dove, Common	*Columbina passerina*
Ground-Dove, Friendly	*Gallicolumba stairi*
Hawk, Ferruginous	*Buteo regalis*
Hawk, Harris's	*Parabuteo unicinctus*
Hawk, Short-tailed	*Buteo brachyurus*
Hawk, Swainson's	*Buteo swainsoni*
Hawk, White-tailed	*Buteo albicaudatus*
Heron, Little Blue	*Egretta caerulea*
Hummingbird, Allen's	*Selasphorus sasin*
Hummingbird, Blue-throated	*Lampornis clemenciae*
Hummingbird, Buff-bellied	*Amazilia yucatanensis*
Hummingbird, Calliope	*Stellula calliope*
Hummingbird, Costa's	*Calypte costae*
Hummingbird, Lucifer	*Calothorax lucifer*
Hummingbird, Rufous	*Selasphorus rufus*
Iiwi	*Vestiaria coccinea*

Jay, Pinyon	*Gymnorhinus cyanocephalus*
Kestrel, American	*Falco sparverius paulus*
Kingbird, Loggerhead	*Tyrannus caudifasciatus*
Kite, Mississippi	*Ictinia mississippiensis*
Kite, Swallow-tailed	*Elanoides forficatus*
Kittiwake, Red-legged	*Rissa brevirostris*
Knot, Red	*Calidris canutu roselaari*
Knot, Red	*Calidris canutus rufa*
Lark, Horned	*Eremophila alpestris strigata*
Limpkin	*Aramus guarauna*
Longspur, Chestnut-collared	*Calcarius ornatus*
Longspur, McCown's	*Calcarius mccownii*
Longspur, Smith's	*Calcarius pictus*
Loon, Red-throated	*Gavia stellata*
Loon, Yellow-billed	*Gavia adamsii*
Magpie, Yellow-billed	*Pica nuttalli*
Mango, Antillean	*Anthracothorax dominicus*
Monarch, Tinian	*Monarcha takatsukasae*
Murrelet, Kittlitz's	*Brachyramphus brevirostris*
Murrelet, Marbled	*Brachyramphus marmoratus*
Murrelet, Xantus's	*Synthliboramphus hypoleucus*
Myzomela, Micronesian	*Myzomela rubrata*
Night-Heron, Black-crowned	*Nycticorax nycticorax*
Nuthatch, Brown-headed	*Sitta pusilla*
Omao	*Myadestes obscurus*
Oriole, Altamira	*Icterus gularis*
Oriole, Audubon's	*Icterus graduacauda*
Oriole, Greater Antillean	*Icterus dominicensis*
Oriole, Hooded	*Icterus cucullatus*
Oriole, Orchard	*Icterus spurius*
Owl, Burrowing	*Athene cunicularia*
Owl, Elf	*Micrathene whitneyi*
Owl, Flammulated	*Otus flammeolus*
Owl, Northern Saw-whet	*Aegolius acadicus*
Owl, Short-eared	*Asio flammeus*
Owl, Spotted	*Strix occidentalis occidentalis*
Oystercatcher, American	*Haematopus palliatus palliatus*
Oystercatcher, Black	*Haematopus bachmani*
Parakeet, Green	*Aratinga holochlora*
Parrot, Red-crowned	*Amazona viridigenalis*
Parula, Tropical	*Parula pitiayumi*
Petrel, Black-capped	*Pterodroma hasitata*
Petrel, Herald	*Pterodroma arminjoniana*
Petrel, Phoenix	*Pterodroma alba*
Petrel, Tahiti	*Pterodroma rostrata*
Phainopepla	*Phainopepla nitens*
Pigeon, Red-billed	*Columba flavirostris*

Pigeon, White-crowned	*Columba leucocephala*
Pintail, White-cheeked	*Anas bahamensis*
Pipit, Sprague's	*Anthus spragueii*
Plover, Mountain	*Charadrius montanus*
Plover, Snowy	*Charadrius alexandrinus nivosus/tenuirostris*
Plover, Wilson's	*Charadrius wilsonia wilsonia*
Prairie-Chicken, Lesser	*Tympanuchus pallidicinctus*
Quail-Dove, Bridled	*Geotrygon mystacea*
Rail, Black	*Laterallus jamaicensis*
Rail, Yellow	*Coturnicops noveboracensis*
Rosy-Finch, Black	*Leucosticte atrata*
Rosy-Finch, Brown-capped	*Leucosticte australis*
Sage-Grouse, Greater	*Centrocerus urophasianus*
Sage-Grouse, Gunnison	*Centrocercus minimus*
Sandpiper, Buff-breasted	*Tryngites subruficollis*
Sandpiper, Purple	*Calidris maritima maritima/belcheri*
Sandpiper, Rock	*Calidris ptilocnemis ptilocnemis*
Sandpiper, Semipalmated	*Calidris pusilla*
Sandpiper, Solitary	*Tringa solitaria*
Sandpiper, Upland	*Bartramia longicauda*
Sapsucker, Williamson's	*Sphyrapicus thyroideus*
Sapsucker, Yellow-bellied	*Sphyrapicus varius*
Scrub-Jay, Island	*Aphelocoma insularis*
Seedeater, White-collared	*Sporophila torqueola*
Shearwater, Audubon's	*Puffinus nativitatis*
Shearwater, Black-vented	*Puffinus opisthomelas*
Shearwater, Christmas	*Puffinus nativitatis*
Shearwater, Greater	*Puffinus gravis*
Shearwater, Pink-footed	*Puffinus creatopus*
Shrike, Loggerhead	*Lanius ludovicianus*
Shrikebill, Fiji	*Clytorhynchus vitiensis*
Skimmer, Black	*Rynchops niger*
Sparrow, Bachman's	*Aimophila aestivalis*
Sparrow, Baird's	*Ammodramus bairdii*
Sparrow, Black-chinned	*Spizella atrogularis*
Sparrow, Botteri's	*Aimophila botterii*
Sparrow, Brewer's	*Spizella breweri*
Sparrow, Cassin's	*Aimophila cassinii*
Sparrow, Field	*Spizella pusilla*
Sparrow, Five-striped	*Aimophila quinquestriata*
Sparrow, Grasshopper	*Ammodramus savannarum*
Sparrow, Grasshopper	*Ammodramus savannarum ammolegus*
Sparrow, Harris's	*Zonotrichia querula*
Sparrow, Henslow's	*Ammodramus henslowii*
Sparrow, Le Conte's	*Ammodramus leconteii*
Sparrow, Nelson's Sharp-tailed	*Ammodramus nelsoni*
Sparrow, Rufous-crowned	*Aimophila ruficeps*

Sparrow, Rufous-winged	*Aimophila carpalis*
Sparrow, Sage	*Amphispiza belli*
Sparrow, Saltmarsh Sharp-tailed	*Ammodramus caudacutus*
Sparrow, Seaside	*Ammodramus maritimus*
Sparrow, Song	*Melospiza melodia graminea*
Sparrow, Song	*Melospiza melodia maxillaris*
Sparrow, Song	*Melospiza melodia pusillula*
Sparrow, Song	*Melospiza melodia samuelis*
Sparrow, Oregon Vesper	*Pooecetes gramineus affinis*
Spoonbill, Roseate	*Platalea ajaja*
Starling, Micronesia	*Aplonis opaca guami*
Starling, Polynesian	*Aplonis tabuensis*
Storm-Petrel, Ashy	*Oceanodroma homochroa*
Storm-Petrel, Band-rumped	*Oceanodroma castro*
Storm-Petrel, Polynesian	*Nesofregatta fuliginosa*
Storm-Petrel, Tristram's	*Oceanodroma tristrami*
Swamphen, Purple	*Porphyrio porphyrio*
Swift, Black	*Cypseloides niger*
Tanager, Summer	*Piranga rubra*
Tern, Caspian	*Hydroprogne caspia*
Tern, Aleutian	*Sterna aleutica*
Tern, Arctic	*Sterna paradisaea*
Tern, Black	*Chlidonias niger*
Tern, Common	*Sterna hirundo*
Tern, Gull-billed	*Gelochelidon nilotica*
Tern, Least	*Sternula antillarum*
Tern, Sandwich	*Thalasseus sandvicensis*
Thrasher, Bendire's	*Toxostoma bendirei*
Thrasher, Brown	*Toxostoma rufum*
Thrasher, Curve-billed	*Toxostoma curvirostre*
Thrasher, Le Conte's	*Toxostoma lecontei*
Thrasher, Sage	*Oreoscoptes montanus*
Thrush, Bicknell's	*Catharus bicknelli*
Thrush, Wood	*Hylocichla mustelina*
Titmouse, Juniper	*Baeolophus ridgwayi*
Titmouse, Oak	*Baeolophus inornatus*
Towhee, Canyon	*Pipilo fuscus*
Towhee, Green- tailed	*Pipilo chlorurus*
Towhee, Spotted	*Pipilo maculates clementae*
Trogon, Elegant	*Trogon elegans*
Verdin	*Auriparus flaviceps*
Veery	*Catharus fuscescens*
Vireo, Bell's	*Vireo bellii*
Vireo, Black-whiskered	*Vireo altiloquus*
Vireo, Gray	*Vireo vicinior*
Vireo, Puerto Rican	*Vireo latimeri*
Warbler, Bay-breasted	*Dendroica castanea*

Warbler, Black-throated-green	*Dendroica virens*
Warbler, Black-throated Gray	*Dendroica nigrescens*
Warbler, Blue-winged	*Vermivora pinus*
Warbler, Canada	*Wilsonia canadensis*
Warbler, Cerulean	*Dendroica cerulea*
Warbler, Colima	*Vermivora crissalis*
Warbler, Elfin-wood	*Dendroica angelae*
Warbler, Golden-winged	*Vermivora chrysoptera*
Warbler, Grace's	*Dendroica graciae*
Warbler, Kentucky	*Oporornis formosus*
Warbler, Lucy's	*Vermivora luciae*
Warbler, Olive	*Peucedramus taeniatus*
Warbler, Prairie	*Dendroica discolor*
Warbler, Prothonotary	*Protonotaria citrea*
Warbler, Red-faced	*Cardellina rubrifrons*
Warbler, Swainson's	*Limnothlypis swainsonii*
Warbler, Virginia's	*Vermivora virginiae*
Warbler, Worm-eating	*Helmitheros vermivorus*
Warbler, Yellow	*Dendroica petechia brewsteri*
Warbler, Yellow	*Dendroica petechia gundlachi*
Warbler, Yellow	*Dendroica petechia sonorana*
Waterthrush, Louisiana	*Seiurus motacilla*
Whimbrel	*Numenius phaeopus*
Whip-poor-will	*Caprimulgus vociferus*
Whistling-Duck, West Indian	*Dendrocygna arborea*
White-eye, Bridled	*Zosterops conspicillatus saypani*
White-eye, Golden	*Cleptornis marchei*
Woodpecker, Arizona	*Picoides arizonae*
Woodpecker, Gila	*Melanerpes uropygialis*
Woodpecker, Lewis's	*Melanerpes lewis*
Woodpecker, Nutall's	*Picoides nuttallii*
Woodpecker, Red-headed	*Melanerpes erythrocephalus*
Woodpecker, White-headed	*Picoides albolarvatus*
Wren, Bewick's	*Thryomanes bewickii bewickii*
Wren, Cactus	*Campylorhynchus brunneicapillus*
Wren, Marsh	*Cistothorus palustris*
Wren, Sedge	*Cistothorus platensis*
Yellowlegs, Lesser	*Tringa flavipes*
Yellowthroat, Common	*Geothlypis trichas sinuosa*